MARCO POLO

Insider Tips

AMSTERDAM

DENMARK
Copenhagen
North Sea
Hamburg
Amsterdam
Berlin
GREAT BRITAIN
NETHER-LANDS
GERMANY
London
English Channel
Brussels
BELGIUM
Frankfurt
LUX.
Paris
FRANCE

www.marco-polo.com

← INSIDE FRONT COVER:
THE BEST HIGHLIGHTS

The best Insider Tips → p. 4

INSIDER TIP

Best of ... → p. 6

Sightseeing → p. 26

Food & drink → p. 56

4 THE BEST INSIDER TIPS

6 BEST OF ...
● GREAT PLACES FOR FREE p. 6
● ONLY IN AMSTERDAM p. 7
● AND IF IT RAINS? p. 8
● RELAX AND CHILL OUT p. 9

10 INTRODUCTION

16 WHAT'S HOT

18 IN A NUTSHELL

24 THE PERFECT DAY

26 SIGHTSEEING
A SURVEY OF AMSTERDAM, DE
WALLEN, CANAL RING & JORDAAN,
WATERLOOPLEIN & PLANTAGE,
OUD ZUID & DE PIJP, MORE SIGHTS,
AROUND AMSTERDAM

56 FOOD & DRINK
AMSTERDAM'S GASTRONOMIC SCENE IS
AS MULTI-CULTURAL AS ITS POPULATION

68 SHOPPING
LOTS OF LITTLE SHOPS:
AMSTERDAM IS RETAIL HEAVEN

SYMBOLS

INSIDER TIP Insider Tip
★ Highlight
●●●● Best of ...
☼ Scenic view
☺ Responsible travel: for
ecological or fair trade
aspects
(*) Telephone numbers that
are not toll-free

PRICE CATEGORIES HOTELS

Expensive	over 170 euros
Moderate	120–170 euros
Budget	under 120 euros

Prices are for one night for a
double room with breakfast

PRICE CATEGORIES RESTAURANTS

Expensive	over 35 euros
Moderate	20–35 euros
Budget	under 20 euros

Prices are for a set menu
without drinks

On the cover: explore the Canal Ring by night p. 80 | Architects' playground p. 53, 98

CONTENTS

ENTERTAINMENT **76**
BORRELUUR, MUSIC AND
CANAL TRIPS

WHERE TO STAY **84**
IN AMSTERDAM ROOMS ARE NOT CHEAP,
BUT THEY HAVE CHARM

WALKING TOURS 94

TRAVEL WITH KIDS 100

FESTIVALS & EVENTS 102

LINKS, BLOGS, APPS & MORE 104

TRAVEL TIPS 106

USEFUL PHRASES 112

STREET ATLAS 118

INDEX & CREDITS 138

DOS & DON'TS! 140

Shopping → p. 68

Entertainment → p. 76

Where to stay → p. 84

Street atlas → p. 118

DID YOU KNOW?
Curtain up! → p. 23
Relax & enjoy → p. 32
Ajax → p. 40
Keep fit! → p. 43
Jewish life → p. 45
Immigrants in the park → p. 53
Local specialities → p. 60
Gourmet restaurants → p. 62
Books & films → p. 82
Luxury hotels → p. 88
Currency converter → p. 107

MAPS IN THE GUIDEBOOK
(120 A1) Page numbers
and coordinates refer to the
street atlas and the map of
Amsterdam and surrounding
area → p. 130/131
(0) Site/address located off
the map. Coordinates are also
given for places, that are not
marked on the street atlas
A public transportation route
map can be found inside the
back cover

INSIDE BACK COVER:
PULL-OUT MAP →

PULL-OUT MAP 𝄜
(𝄜 A–B 2–3) Refers to the
removable pull-out map

The best
MARCO POLO
Insider Tips

Our top 15 Insider Tips

INSIDER TIP ▶ Hot and crispy

The prawn croquettes, available in the *Holtkamp bakery*, is a city-wide speciality → **p. 23**

INSIDER TIP ▶ Where it's happening

Built as a workers' quarter, today De Pijp is characterised by its mix of student pubs, chic restaurants, market bustle and Asian shops → **p. 49**

INSIDER TIP ▶ Picturesque dyke village

Country feel in the city: today, Nieuwendam is part of Amsterdam, but it has kept its village atmosphere with old wooden houses → **p. 54**

INSIDER TIP ▶ Green surroundings, green cuisine

Organic food in an old, eight-metre-high greenhouse: De Kas serves up modern Dutch food with ingredients from its own garden → **p. 61**

INSIDER TIP ▶ Rent a bike and off you pedal

Experience Amsterdam as the locals do – on a *rented bike* → **p. 106**

INSIDER TIP ▶ Say cheese

Kaashuis Tromp lives up to the clichés: all sorts of cheeses are piled up to the ceiling in this little shop → **p. 70**

INSIDER TIP ▶ Unexpected flavours

Puccini's hand-made chocolates release their very own, surprising flavours with ingredients like nutmeg pepper and gin → **p. 71**

INSIDER TIP ▶ Futuristic footwear

The designer is related to the famous architect Rem Koolhaas, and it does come across in the shoes footwear by United Nude with its creative heel styling is coveted around the world → **p. 74**

INSIDER TIP Outdoors and free
If you attend one of the many summer concerts in Amsterdam's Vondelpark, you are often treated to a spontaneous and carefree open-air after party → **p. 102**

INSIDER TIP Bar with a view
Watch the sunset from the *Skylounge* in the Doubletree hotel on Oosterdokseiland with a breathtaking view of the old city, the harbour and IJ → **p. 77**

INSIDER TIP Open-air museum
Steamers once set off for Sumatra from the Oostelijke Haven islands; today this is a showcase for contemporary Dutch architecture → **p. 98**

INSIDER TIP Secret church in the attic
The name says it all: 'our dear Lord in the attic' is the name of the canal house. In its attic you can visit the *secret church* → **p. 35**

INSIDER TIP Bobbing bungalows
Amsterdam's houseboats are certainly pretty to look at. But if you really want to experience life on the water, with all the splashing, rocking and bobbing up and down, then book one for a night. Or two or three ... (photo below) → **p. 85**

INSIDER TIP Start the day in style
Palms, chandeliers and murals beneath a ceiling of glass: nowhere in Amsterdam is a good breakfast more stylish than in the wonderful winter garden of the Krasnapolsky luxury hotel → **p. 86**

INSIDER TIP Design in your room
Once a hostel where a shipping line accommodated emigrants before their departure for a new life overseas, now home to art and design. The individually styled rooms of the magnificent Lloyd Hotel guarantee an unconventional overnight stay → **p. 89**

BEST OF ...

FOR FREE

● *Paintings of the Guard*
In a covered alley behind Kalverstraat, in *Schuttersgalerij*, 15 enormous group portraits of the Civic Guard from the Golden Age are on display with no admission charge → p. 29

● *Park life*
Amsterdam's place to meet in summer is Vondelpark (photo). Visit one of the many free open-air concerts, have a picnic or play football. This park is a magnet for social gatherings rather than a place for peace and quiet → p. 52

● *Midday classics*
The lunch-time concerts in the Concertgebouw are an Amsterdam institution – and there is no admission charge. Every Wednesday at 12.30pm you can enjoy a rehearsal of the Concertgebouw Orchestra or listen to a half-hour concert by talented young musicians → p. 82

● *Open-air cinema*
The *Pluk de Nacht* film festival held out of doors on a small peninsula on Westerdoksdijk runs over several weeks in August. You only have to pay if you want a warm blanket to go with your deckchair → p. 103

● *Galleries in Jordaan*
If you want to catch up on some contemporary art, you don't always have to buy a ticket: the alternative is a wander through the galleries of Amsterdam. Most of the renowned galleries, for example *Fons Welters, Annet Gelink* or *Torch* are situated close together in the Jordaan district → p. 40, 71

● *As colourful as it gets*
The Chinese like things to be colourful. Among all the old brick buildings on Zeedijk stands the Buddhist Fo Guang Shan He Hua Temple, where you can catch a glimpse of the religious heart of Amsterdam's China-town → p. 32

○○○●● Dots in guidebook refer to 'Best of ...' tips

ONLY IN AMSTERDAM
Unique experiences

● *Cycle city*
You can't imagine Amsterdam without bicycles. Thanks
to many hire stations, visitors can pedal around just
as the locals do. At *Star Bikes Rental* the service
is extremely friendly, and they'll even do you a
good latte macchiato → p. 106

● *Life on the canal*
The houses on Amsterdam's canals (canal
= 'gracht') can be crooked and leaning to
one side, or imposing and elegant. Lining
the canals of the old part of town, shoulder
to shoulder, they were all built of brick, but
when you look more closely, no two are alike.
The finest residences are in the *Gouden Bocht*
(Golden Arc) on Herengracht → p. 41

● *Brown cafés*
They have to be wood-panelled all round, but above all cosy and
sociable: the 'brown cafés' that you find on almost every corner in
Amsterdam. Some examples of this type of establishment, like *De
Oosterling* or *'t Smalle,* are several hundred years old → p. 78, 96

● *Royal date*
Since Beatrix's abdication in 2013 the former *Koninginnedag* has
become a *Koningsdag*. On this day, the 27th April, everyone in the
Netherlands celebrates their King Willem-Alexander. The day begins
with a city-wide flea market which then turns into a street party towards the afternoon. This is not only an opportunity to get dressed
in orange from head to toe but to also push the boat out → p. 102

● *Bridges everywhere*
In the historic parts of the city there are no less than 600 bridges
(photo), the most famous of which is the *Magere Brug* across the Amstel. At the junction of Reguliersgracht and Herengracht you can even
take in 15 bridges all at once → p. 42

● *All around the globe*
The shelves are filled with foodstuffs from Thailand, Surinam and India,
and salsa music pours from the hi-fi system. If you want to see how
cosmopolitan Amsterdam is, peek inside one of the *tokos,* the little
shops that sell exotic provisions, for example around Albert Cuypmarkt
→ p. 69

ONLY IN

BEST OF ...

● *A new kind of library*
In the public *Openbare Bibliotheek* you can not only read books but also walk around, admire the furnishings made by Dutch designers, surf the internet for free, listen to music, leaf through international newspapers and have a coffee → **p. 35**

● *Underwater worlds*
A zoo is not the obvious place to go in bad weather, but *Artis* is a different matter. This historic aquarium shows you life under the seas, and there is also a butterfly pavilion with colourful butterflies → **p. 100**

● *Cosy cinema*
The Movies on Haarlemmerdijk is Amsterdam's oldest cinema and has retained its Art Deco styling. After the film stay for a beer in the cosy cinema pub → **p. 81**

● *Shopping in the post office*
The *Magna Plaza* shopping centre was built in the late 19th century as the main post office. Today this imposing Gothic Revival building houses upmarket fashion stores and cafés around its spacious court-yards → **p. 68**

● *A trip overseas*
The Tropenmuseum (photo) brings to life the colonial history of the Netherlands and also conveys an impression of life in far-away coun-tries today – including a storm in the African savannah and a boat trip through the rainforest → **p. 49**

● *From the city hall to the palace*
King Willem-Alexander rarely stays in the *Koninklijk Paleis*, which was originally built as a city hall. All the same, its impressive rooms are well worth seeing – especially the Great Hall, which depicts the universe with Amsterdam at its centre → **p. 32**

RAIN

RELAX AND CHILL OUT
Take it easy and spoil yourself

● *Art Deco sauna*

The *Sauna Déco* lies right on Herengracht. This 600 m² sauna complex has been furnished with the Art Deco interior of a Paris department store that was demolished. The leaded-light windows and ornamental lamps make it a particularly good place to relax → **p. 32**

● *Hippy paradise*

Blijburg aan Zee, on the eastern edge of the newly built IJburg quarter, is a habitat for hippies. In summer abandon yourself to the lazy pleasures of sunshine and water on this nicely improvised city beach → **p. 54**

● *Just swim*

Amsterdam's most attractive swimming bath, the *Zuiderbad,* has little to offer apart from a single pool in a historic building. But that is exactly what makes it so relaxing: you can come here simply to swim in peace → **p. 43**

● *A green spa*

'Zuiver' is the Dutch word for 'clean', and a stay at the *Hotel Spa Zuiver* is guaranteed to make you just that. On the edge of the Amsterdamse Bos woodland, it offers a spa holiday in the south of the city – with or without an overnight stay → **p. 90**

● *A cosy café*

The *Nemo Science Center* in the Oosterdok (photo) looks like a beached whale. You can walk up the terraced back of the building, and in summer there is an open-air café at the top with beanbags for seats and a fantastic view across the historic city. Parents can sip a glass of rosé while their children play in the paddling pool → **p. 100**

● *A dyked village in the city*

If you are looking for a refuge from Amsterdam's hectic life, board bus no. 32 at the main station and go to Nieuwendammerdijk. On the other side of the river IJ you will suddenly find that you are in an ancient dyked village → **p. 54**

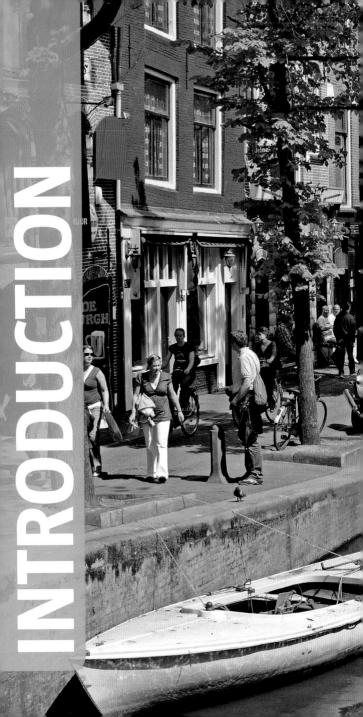

INTRODUCTION

DISCOVER AMSTERDAM!

The narrow-fronted houses lean on each other at a slight angle. A cyclist crosses a bridge on his squeaking bike, and outside the café on the corner, people sit in the sun enjoying a cup of coffee. In the distance you can hear a tram rumbling across Leidseplein. ‚A beautiful city, Amsterdam. Even an exile can admire the noble simplicity of the architecture of the old patricians' houses and sense the sequestered charm of the canals with their Venetian smells and perspectives', as Klaus Mann wrote in the 1930s. And today millions of visitors fall for the charm of the city on the Amstel just as this German writer did 80 years ago.

No wonder: Amsterdam is an incredibly diverse city. Old and new, calm and bustling, artistic and commercial, small-town and cosmopolitan atmosphere – there is no way to describe the city without contradictions. With almost 7500 listed buildings, Amsterdam boasts the highest density of historic monuments in the Netherlands. Since 2010 the historic Canal Ring has been a Unescow World Heritage site. In the old core

Photo: The attractions of life on the canals – narrow façades, leafy trees, old boats on Oudezijds Achterburgwal of the city there is something historic to discover on every corner, from carved gables to old shipyards and a secret church below the roof of a canalside house.

Almost half the population is under 35 years of age

As its centre is compact, Amsterdam, which is built on more than 90 islands, is a wonderful city for strolling about. Only by walking along the brick-paved little streets by the canals can you take in the elegance of the tall, narrow-fronted burghers' houses, spot the heron on the roof of a houseboat, or discover here and there a hidden courtyard or a little antique shop. The historic ensemble of the Canal Ring has been preserved in its entirety over centuries. For this reason the whole city centre was given protected status in 1999. And in other districts too, for example villagey Jordaan, time seems to have stood still.

The fact that Amsterdam is nevertheless no lifeless open-air museum but a vibrant city has to do on the one hand with the relaxed attitude of the Dutch to their monuments – as in the case of neon signs on a Gothic stepped gable – and on the other hand with its exceptionally cosmopolitan and youthful population. Half of Amsterdam residents do not come from the Netherlands, and 41 per cent of them are under 35 years of age. This is what gives the entertainment quarters around Leidseplein and Rembrandtplein such a buzz, makes the range of shopping options unlimited, and

Kalverstraat: a shopping street where you see faces from every continent

means that guests at the countless restaurants are faced with a tantalising choice of specialities.

Amsterdam is appealing at any time of the year – in summer, when the cafés put tables out on the street and an almost Mediterranean atmosphere prevails, or in winter, when the canals are veiled in mist and the bridges sport pretty illuminations. Its main attractions include three major museums, the Rijksmuseum, Van Gogh Museum and Stedelijk Museum with their unique art treasures, and the numerous little shops, *winkels,* in the city centre. And the popularity of Amsterdam as a destination for visitors from all over the world is also down to the open and good-natured character of its people.

The mentality of the Amsterdamers, their commercial spirit and proverbial tolerance, have had a decisive influence on the history of the city. It originated as a marshy fishing village at the point where the river Amstel flowed into the IJsselmeer, which is now a lake but was then part

> **A commercial spirit and proverbial tolerance**

of the North Sea. In 1275 the village of Amstelledamme was granted freedom from customs duties, gained a town charter in 1300 and from then onwards thanks to its location controlled the flow of goods between the North Sea and the Dutch hinterland. The commercially minded Amsterdamers were always on the lookout for new opportunities: it was not long before they were trading with the whole of the Baltic Sea and the North Sea regions. To protect themselves against high tides, they started to construct a line of defences, the *wallen.* The oldest quarter of the city between Oudezijds and Nieuwezijds Achterburgwal, which has to a large extent been preserved, is today Chinatown and the red-light district.

At the end of the 16th century the northern Netherlands freed themselves from Spanish rule in the 80 Years War. In this period Amsterdam gained an early reputation for being liberal, and attracted many Protestant and Jewish refugees from places like Antwerp and Lisbon, which were still ruled by Spain. These waves of immigration by wealthy merchants extended trade connections and ushered in the so-called Golden Age. In 1602 the Dutch East India Company (Verenigde Oostindische Compagnie, VOC) was established with a monopoly of maritime trade with the Far East and India, and in 1621 the Westindische Compagnie was founded to carry on trade with America and the west coast of Africa. Over the following 150 years the Netherlands became one of the leading European naval and commercial powers, and Amsterdam grew to be a rich and important port, its warehouses filled with cloves, cinnamon, silk, coffee and porcelain. Within a few decades the number of residents increased by a factor of five.

In the early 17th century, with the city bursting at the seams, construction was started of concentric rings of canals: outside the old *wallen*, rich merchants built fine residences with attached warehouses on Herengracht, Keizersgracht or Prinsengracht. The arts and literature flowered at the same time. The greatest works of the Golden

Age such as Rembrandt's Nightwatch and Vermeer's Kitchen Maid can be admired in the Rijksmuseum today – testimony to a bourgeois Protestant culture in which commercial shrewdness and openness to the world formed a fruitful combination.

Around 1700 Amsterdam boasted approximately 220,000 inhabitants and had reached the peak of its prosperity. By 1750 the great age of the Netherlands had already passed. This was partly the result of the increasing strength of other maritime powers such as England, but was also due to the bureaucratic management style of the VOC. Only in the mid-19th century did the economy recover thanks to industrialisation and the construction of the Nordzeekanal, which enabled ocean-going ships to enter the port of Amsterdam.

> Coffee shops and homosexual partnerships give the city a certain image

In the Second World War the Netherlands fell to German forces after five days of fighting. The speed of the capitulation meant that Amsterdam suffered little damage, although it was later hit several times by misdirected Allied bombing. Resistance to the German occupation formed, but was not able to prevent the almost complete annihilation of the Jewish community.

In the 1970s Amsterdam was a mecca for hippies, squatters and drop-outs from all over the world. Thousands of backpackers camped out in Vondelpark and on the Dam in summer, and by 1980 the population of the city included some 20,000 squatters. Liberal politicians achieved the legalisation of soft drugs, and every marginal group was free to do its own thing. Today this reputation still clings to Amsterdam – not just tulips and canals, but also 'coffee shops' where drugs can be consumed freely and civil partnerships for homosexuals.

A few years ago, however, a change in mentality took place, and the Dutch became noticeably more conservative. The conservative liberal party VVD is the strongest party in parliament, squatting was made illegal at the end of 2010. Since then, in coffee shops along the border provinces only costumers with a Dutch residency pass are allowed to enter. Amsterdam however is an exception to this rule. Despite the growing criticism in the canal city towards the ineffective integration and high unemployment rates among the Moroccan and Turkish immigrants, the social democrats hold the majority in the city council and coffeeshops are open to everyone. The prohibition on squatting has been implemented, however, so that occupied houses, known as *kraakpand* and once a familiar sight all over the city, are becoming increasingly rare.

By way of contrast, cranes and building sites are more and more common. A lot has happened in recent years, especially on the banks of the IJ. Whereas completely new quarters of the city have risen up in the former dockland area to the east of the main station, construction work around the new *Eye Filminstitut* on the north bank and in the old timber docks to the west of the inner city is still going ahead. From north to south, too, a conspicuous chain of building sites crosses the city: it is planned to open a new underground line in 2017.

> **Compact, remarkably laid-back, sometimes chaotic**

In the historic centre you don't notice much of all this. Amsterdam is and will remain a compact, remarkably laid-back, sometimes rather chaotic metropolis with about 790,000 inhabitants. Amsterdamers' preferred means of transport is still the ecologically correct *fiets* (bicycle), usually rusty. On summer weekends a popular activity is to chug along the canals in little boats drinking a glass of rosé, or to sit in the sun with a cup of coffee on the pavement in front of the house. Cafés are an important part of everyday life. Whether dark pubs, cool design bars or candle-lit snugs – what matters is that they are *gezellig*, cosy and sociable.

Thanks to its enormous diversity, Amsterdam attracts many different kinds of visitors. But when the elms are reflected in the water of the canals and the glockenspiel of the Westerkerk chimes in the background, they are all equally fascinated.

Take a boat to your own front door: water is the dominant element in this city

WHAT'S HOT

1 Home cooking

Private dinner They invite you into their own flat and serve a meal on grandmother's dinner service. Home cooking is all the rage in Amsterdam. One of the foremost exponents is Marit Beemster with her *Huiskamerrestaurant (Andreas Bonnstraat 34h | www.maritshuiskamerrestaurant.nl)*. Adrienne Eisma also invites guests to her home *(The Cookery | Valeriusstraat 250 | www.thecookery.nl)*. At the *Kookerij de Singel (Singel 317 | www.fork spoon.nl)* you can choose between a home-cooked meal and other selected locations.

Recycling art

2

Art Amsterdam's artists are ace recyclers. Leonard van Munster, for example, who balanced a tree house made from rubbish on the *Stedelijk Museum (www.leonardvanmunster.com)* *(photo)*. Robert Pennekamp also makes art out of garbage, collecting materials for a sculpture with the slogan ‚make rubbish into something beautiful' *(www.robertpen nekamp.nl)*. The high point of the annual *Trashville Festival (www.trashville.nl)* is the Trash Race, in which only vehicles built on the spot from waste materials can compete.

3 Spot on

Trendy quarter The lure of the filthy: an increasing number of restraurant and café owners are rediscovering the red-light district. Among the new establishments that are nestled between sex shops and windows of prostitutes are the cosy café and restaurant *Mata Hari (Oudezijds Achterburgwal 22 | www.matahari-amsterdam.nl)*, the *Metropolitan Deli (Warmoesstraat 111 | www.metropolitandeli.nl)* and the renowned *Restaurant Anna (Warmoesstraat 111 | www.restaurantanna.nl)*.

There are lots of new things to discover in Amsterdam. A few of the most interesting are listed below

Go green

Environmentally sound The canals are being given a green makeover. Visitors to Amsterdam can explore its waterways with a clear ecological conscience. Just board the emission-free boat of the *Rederij Lovers (www.lovers.nl) (photo)*. Nemo H2 is powered by a hydrogen-based fuel cell and emits neither noise, nor smell nor exhaust gases. The city's electro-taxis are also kind to the environment. They look like London's black cabs, but purring beneath the bonnet is an electric engine *(www.tcataxi.nl)*. Bus stops, too, have gone green. Utrecht-sestraat has been declared a ‚climate street' and has bus shelters with solar generators that provide power to the advertising displays.

Body and soul

Paddle, float, climb Standup paddleboarding is an almost medita-tive experience. If you don't know the ropes, take part in one of the courses run three times a week by *M & M SUP (www.mm-sup.com) (photo)*. In the summer months they also organise paddling sessions by night, *Night SUP*. If that's not enough to calm you down, try floating. Weightless drifting in a saltwa-ter pool is a great antidote to stress *(Koan Float, Herengracht 321, www.koanfloat.nl)*. One of the winter attractions is the *Jaap Eden* indoor ice rink *(Radioweg 64 | www.jaapeden.nl)* in the suburb of Water-graafsmeer. Iceskating is generally done with long upward curving skates and thus lends the skaters an air of elegance and of endurance . If you want to try them out, you can rent them *(an ID or a deposit of 100 euros is necessary)*.

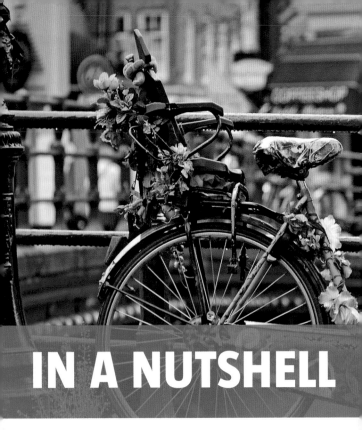

IN A NUTSHELL

BICYCLES

There are said to be more than 550,000 bicycles in Amsterdam. Around one third of the inhabitants always get around this way – in a compact but permanently congested city with few parking spaces, a *fiets* is the best means of transport. Cyclists are allowed to do almost anything, such as riding side by side along the street and transporting passengers on the carrier rack. For some years now there has been a focus on bike lights: checks on cyclists' lights are regularly held in the evenings on the street of Amsterdam. Most bikes in the city are in an awful condition. This is deliberate: if a bike looks too expensive, it will be stolen in next to no time.

CANALS

Amsterdam is inescapably known as the 'Venice of the north'. And canals are indeed a dominant feature of the scene in the historic city centre. Once they had the function of sewers: once a day the sluice gates were opened and the dirty water flowed out into the Zuiderzee, now called the IJsselmeer. Nowadays the water is still circulated several times a week. In the 1960s and 1970s several canals were filled in for the sake of road traffic in the historic centre. Only their names – Vijzelgracht, Lindengracht, Palmgracht – serve as a reminder that these streets were once waterways.

Photo: Bikes and flowers – as typical for Amsterdam as canals and coffee shops

Houseboats, monarchy and snack culture:
What's characteristic, remarkable and
strange in the city of canals

COFFEE SHOPS

The Netherlands is the only country in the world where the public sale of up to 5 grams of cannabis is accepted. All the same, these sales are illegal – they are simply not prosecuted, a contradiction that is accepted according to the Dutch term *gedogen*, which means toleration. This policy is intended to draw a line between the markets for hard and soft drugs. In Amsterdam the latter can be bought and consumed in approximately 100 coffee shops. The menu of these establishments, which are often filled with a pungent aroma, also includes fruit juice or smoothies, but no beer or spirits –a different licence is required to serve alcohol.

DUTCH DESIGN

Dutch design has been on the up since the 1990s. All over the world products by Dutch designers, generally simple but quirky, are much sought after. It all started with *Droog Design* (literally: dry design), a collective of young designers who got together in the mid-1990s in Amsterdam to evolve an alternative to the super-smooth, high-gloss side of the design world. In no time at all their first products – including an armchair made from old clothing bundled together, a chandelier from a bunch of light bulbs and a doorbell made out of two wine glasses – were world-famous.

In the meantime Dutch design has almost become a brand, and Droog Design has opened a popular store-cum-gallery in Staalstraat, where unusual products by young designers are on sale. The most famous internationally of the former Droog designers, Marcel Wanders, is now taking a different path: he has opted for the fanciful forms of neo-Baroque, but does so with tongue in cheek. Since 2009 an old school in Jordaan has been home to his design label *Moooi*. He got the opportunity to move in here thanks to the city council of Amsterdam, which has consciously supported the design business in recent years. This policy has produced festivals such as *Dutch Design Double*, which is held in September each year, and the whole new city library being equipped with Dutch designer furniture. Also, a host of young designers have been established in the red-light district, where studios have been set up in former brothels – which speaks volumes about the way Amsterdam would like to develop as a tourist destination.

FLOWERS

If you are invited to a birthday party or for a meal in Holland, never turn up without a bunch of flowers. For centuries, cut flowers, especially tulips of course, have been part of Dutch culture and an important branch of the economy. Flowers worth eight billion euros are exported annually. On average each Dutch citizen spends 76 euros per year on flowers – a fair sum of money in view of the low prices for a bunch of flowers. There are little flower stalls everywhere in Amsterdam to meet the demand.

HET IJ

A large stretch of water behind the main station, the IJ (pronounced something like ‚aye'), is the northern border of the inner city of Amsterdam. Huge cruise liners come from the North Sea to their terminal through the IJ, cargo ships coming from the Rhine canal head for the port of Amsterdam, and little passenger ferries cross to and fro non-stop to Amsterdam-Noord. It is hard to say exactly what the IJ is. A river? A canal? Part of the sea? A lake? Not of these descriptions really nails it. Before 1932, when the front-line dyke in the north of Holland had not yet been built, the IJsselmeer east of Amsterdam was still the Zuiderzee, part of the North Sea. Het IJ was then an arm of the Zuiderzee, i.e. a bay of sea. It originally terminated in the dunes west of Amsterdam; direct access to the open North Sea was only created in 1876 through the North Sea Canal. At the same time a dam and the Oranje sluices were built in the north of Amsterdam to separate the IJ from the IJsselmeer. Today the IJ is usually described as a river. Its water is slightly salty, but officially is not regarded as seawater. Herring and other sea fish nevertheless feel absolutely at home in it.

HOIST BEAMS

You can see them on almost every house, whether 4 or 400 years old:

Love your houseboat! The Amsterdamers even let their houseboats burst into bloom

beams for a hoist. Usually the beams with their attached hooks stick out from the house fronts above a window in the roof. They are by no means historic artefacts, but are still used today. The stairs in Amsterdam's houses are extremely steep and narrow, which makes it almost impossible to take large items to the upper floors. Instead you borrow a pulley from a removal company, attach it to the beam, hoist up wardrobes, pianos and anything else that is bulky, and haul it into the flat through a window.

HOUSEBOATS

Sometimes they look well kept, sometimes shabby; some are old barges that have been converted, others have the appearance of floating bungalows. 2400 houseboats bob up and down on the city canals, es-

pecially Singel and Prinsengracht. In the 1950s it was students who first hit on the idea that disused boats would make excellent accommodation. The city authorities, however, have always been reluctant to accept these floating domiciles, and it is now practically impossible to get a mooring for a new houseboat.

MONARCHY

The Netherlands are a constitutional monarchy. This has not always been the case: although the house of Orange-Nassau has ruled since 1572, Holland was initially a republic after the wars of liberation against Spain. For some 200 years the Orange dynasty only held the position of governor. The first king, Willem I, did not ascend the throne until 1815, after occupation by Napoleon's forces.

In Amsterdam you see three crosses everywhere: on coats of arms, crowns and souvenirs

It may seem surprising that of all people the pragmatic Dutch allow themselves the luxury of a royal family. But just like her mother Juliana, who died in 2004 and was known to be particularly close to her people, Queen Beatrix (born 1938), who succeeded to the throne in 1980 and abdicated in 2013, is very popular with the people of the Netherlands. Her son Willem-Alexander (born 1967) is now King of the Netherlands. When he was younger he had a reputation as party animal, and that earned him the nickname *prins pils*. This however changed when he married the Argentinian commoner Máxima Zorreguieta (born 1971). Currently, Queen Máxima is almost as popular as her mother-in-law. Whenever the royal couple and their three daughters Amalia (born 2003), Alexia (born 2005) und Ariane (born 2007) make an appearance on television, the viewing figures hit high levels.

SNACKING

Kroket, frikandel, loempia and *patat oorlog* – these are the stars of Amsterdam's snacking scene. All of them deep-fried and deliciously unhealthy. Some, like *loempia* (a cigar-shaped spring roll with hot and sweet chilli sauce), *bamischijf* (spicy noodles, deep-fried and pressed into disk shape) and *patat oorlog* (French fries with mayonnaise, peanut sauce and onions) reveal gastronomic influences from the Dutch colonial past.

But *nieuwe haring* (lightly salted herring, also known as matjes), which is as Dutch as Dutch can be, is also part of a flourishing fast-food culture, as it is seldom eaten as a main course but usually as a snack in-between taken at a stall on the street. The zenith of Amsterdam's culture of snacking is the *automatiek,* a machine for selling hot and greasy foodstuffs. Behind little doors cheese soufflés, meatballs and noodle disks are waiting for someone to throw a few euros into the slot, open the door and devour them. The best-known chain of snack bars with *automatiek* is called *Febo,* was founded as long ago as 1941 and is represented on almost every corner in Amsterdam. Connoisseurs swear by the home-made `INSIDER TIP` *shrimp and meat croquettes of the Holtkamp bakery* at number 15 Vijzelgracht, which can also be found among the starters on menus in good restaurants.

X **XX**

In many places in Amsterdam you see a symbol consisting of three crosses, one above the other. It adorns not only the crown at the tip of the Westertoren, but also the gables of canal-side houses and above all the little brown posts known as Amsterdammertjes that separate the pavement from the road in the city centre. Some visitors speculate that these crosses have something to do with the red-light district and X-rated films – and in many shops you can buy humorous souvenirs that play on this association. In reality however they are the three St Andrew's crosses, which have been part of the city coat of arms since the Middle Ages. It is not clear why the coat of arms features these three crosses. It may be connected to the fact that most Amsterdamers were fisherman then, like St Andrew. From 1505 all ships registered in Amsterdam were required to fly the flag with the three crosses.

CURTAIN UP!

Windows three metres high without curtains are not an unusual sight on Amsterdam's canals. Many visitors express surprise at the openness of the Dutch, while others tell of a historic tax on curtains that cause the thrifty Amsterdamers to do without. This tax is pure myth. It is true that there was a window tax in the 19th century, but this was only related to the number of windows, not how they were decorated. It is more probable that the way the houses on canals were constructed made curtains unnecessary. On the street side of the raised ground floor there was usually a reception room designed to impress guests, into which passers-by were welcome to look. The private living rooms lay behind it, shielded from prying eyes. Others attribute the lack of curtains to the Calvinist religion: a good Calvinist had nothing to hide and therefore let everyone look inside his home. In view of the high-class designer furniture that can often be seen behind the glass in expensive houses on the canals, the owners' pride in their possessions might also be an explanation. However, they only attract the attention of foreign visitors, as one of the Calvinist rules of the game is that the Dutch themselves never stare through other peoples' windows, however open to public gaze they may be.

THE PERFECT DAY
Amsterdam in 24 hours

10:00am **BETWEEN CANAL RING AND WESTERKERK**

Amsterdamers are definitely not early risers — and there are benefits to that, as you have the city to yourself early in the morning. The ideal day in Amsterdam doesn't start until 10 o'clock, e.g. with a light breakfast in the café *Spanjer & van Twist* → p. 58. In summer if you drink your *koffie verkeerd* (coffee with milk) and croissant on the sunny little terrace on Leliegracht, you really have a front-row seat. After that it's time for a stroll around the *Canal Ring* → p. 38. It takes no more than a short walk on Herengracht (photo l.), Brouwersgracht and Keizersgracht to get an impression of the unique architecture of the bridges and brick-built houses of the Golden Age. Thanks to the famous *absence of curtains* → p. 23 you can also glimpse marble-clad interiors with plasterwork ceilings. If you feel like it, go as far as *Jordaan* → p. 94, once a poor district, with its narrow streets and village atmosphere. Continue to the *Westerkerk* → p. 44, as in summer you can linger on this church tower enjoying the bird's-eye view of the maze of streets and houses of the almost completely preserved old quarter of Amsterdam. You can rent a pedal boat at the foot of the Westerkerk and enjoy an hourly view of the canals.

12:00pm **SEE SOME MASTERPIECES**

A short walk along leafy Bloemgracht, where Rembrandt once lived, leads to the stop for tram number 10, which goes to the *Rijksmuseum* → p. 50. After extensive renovations the Museum was reopened in 2013 and it's former splendour can once again be admired. Its historical halls transport the visitor back into the Golden Age. It is above all small, inconspicuous genre paintings like Jan Steen's The Morning Toilet, showing a young woman taking off her stockings, that bring the 17th century to life in an astonishing way.

02:00pm **BUSTLING MARKET LIFE**

If all this culture has given you an appetite, it's fortunately not far to *Albert Cuypmarkt* → p. 72 (photo right): from the southern end of Museumplein the tram goes into Albert Cuypstraat. On the open-air market in the hip De Pijp quarter you fill up on local favourites such as matjes herring or French fries, while market traders shout out the praises of their wares in Amsterdam dialect, women from Surinam haggle over the price of sweet potatoes and young parents push designer prams through the crowds.

Discover Amsterdam at its best: in the thick of things, relaxed – and all in a single day

`03:30pm` SHOPPING STREET

From the eastern end of the market it's a cobblestone's throw to *Utrechtsestraat* → p. 68 with its attractive shops and cafés. This is just the place for a short shopping tour, as you find everything here from designer fashion and underwear to cheese and CDs. However, bring enough money with you, as this street is close to the upmarket historic canal area.

`05:30pm` BEER, BITTERBALLEN AND RIJSTAFEL

In the evening, brown cafés like *Wynand Fockink* → p. 79 get crowded with office workers who come here for their *borrel,* which usually consists of a beer with *bitterballen*. Don't eat too many of them, but leave room for your evening meal. In the restaurant *Hotel de Goudfazant* → p. 61 in the dockland area to the north the creative scene meets for modern Dutch cooking. An alternative if you prefer to stay in the city centre is to go to an Indonesian restaurant and treat yourself to *rijsttafel,* a menu consisting of a large number of small, often spicy dishes – not an Indonesian speciality, incidentally, but a Dutch invention.

`11:00pm` CLUBS & CO.

If you're looking for entertainment, then it's best to head for *Nieuwmarkt* → p. 35 (photo above right). There are cafés and pubs all around this square with the Weighing House. Curiosity sends some visitors from here into the red-light district or *Chinatown* → p. 32. For clubs it's better to go to *Leidseplein* → p. 42 or more distant, unexpected venues such as the old newspaper printworks on Wibautstraat, where party people dance in *Club Trouw* → p. 79 to the sounds of international DJs in summer until the sun rises over the roofs of the city.

Tram to the start: 13, 14, 17
Tram stop: Westerkerk
Best time to start: morning

SIGHTSEEING

WHERE TO START?

CITY **WHERE TO START?**
Dam (120 B3) (*∭ F3*): The ideal starting point for exploring Amsterdam. This historic main city square on the main axis running from the main station is the site of the Nationaal Monument, the Royal Palace and the Nieuwe Kerk, but also of the long-established department store Bijenkorf, and is the start of the Kalverstraat shopping street. You can park a car at the Bijenkorf store, but it is cheaper and less stressful to walk five minutes from the station or take a tram; lines 1, 2, 4, 5, 9, 13, 14, 16, 17, 24 and 25 stop at the Dam.

Amsterdam has no fewer than 7500 protected buildings. Most of them are situated within comfortable walking distance of the city centre – either in de Wallen, the oldest district of the city, or in the canal quarter.

No-one should leave Amsterdam without taking a proper walk along Singel, Herengracht, Keizersgracht or Prinsengracht. Some more recent or less well-known quarters of the city are also worth a detour. If you want to get a first overall impression of Amsterdam, go up the ⚡ tower of the Westerkerk.

If you have come to see the highlights of Dutch art, then the decision is easy: the Rijksmuseum, Van Gogh Museum and Stedelijk Museum, the three most important in the country, are all situated on

Photo: Museums, galleries and enchanting gardens can be found behind unassuming façades on the canals

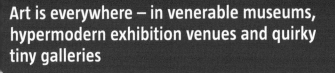

Art is everywhere – in venerable museums, hypermodern exhibition venues and quirky tiny galleries

one square, Museumplein. Due to years of renovations these museums were closed or only partially accessible to the public, but once again visitors can now admire the master pieces of the Golden Age, of impressionism and of modernism. Whereas the Rijksmuseum shines in its former splendour, the Stedelijk Museum was given a new conspicuous annex in the shape of a gigantic bathtub. Irrespective of what your opinion is on that architecture: the quality of the art collection of these three museums is exceptional.

Amsterdam's museums are not only for art lovers. If handbags, history or simply strange and unusual collections are your thing, there is a museum here for you. And if you prefer not to do everything on foot, the *Canal Bus* will take you from door to door, as its three routes include stops at all the important museums. For 22 euros you can hop on and off wherever you want all day and up to noon on the following day, and in addition get a reduced admission charge at a number of museums.

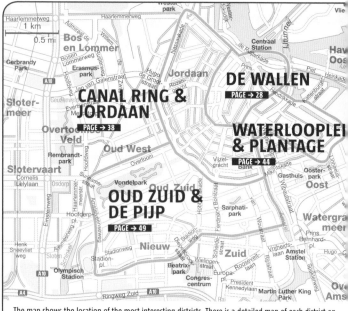

The map shows the location of the most interesting districts. There is a detailed map of each district on which each of the sights described is numbered.

If you plan to visit several museums, it's worth buying a *Museumkaart (MK, www.museumkaart.nl)*. This annual ticket gets you into most of the major museums of the Netherlands. For adults the standard price is 44.90 euros, but those under 24 pay only 24.90 euros. The ticket is on sale in every museum and can be used there straight away. To find out which museums take the *Museumkaart*, in this travel guide you will find the letters MK in brackets next to the admission price.

It is also worth considering the purchase of the *I amsterdam City Card,* which includes admission for two or three days to the best-known museums in Amsterdam as well as covering public transport (p. 111).

DE WALLEN

Amsterdam's medieval centre *De Wallen* takes its name from the four oldest canals in the city: the former defensive moats called Voor- and Achterburgwal, both of which surrounded the 'oude' and 'nieuwe zijde' (the old and the new side) of the city.

Around these canals – of which only two remain, as both watercourses on the 'new side' were filled in – a lively quarter with a colourfully mixed character has grown up. Alongside historic sights and shopping centres it encompasses the red-light district and Chinatown. Here you will find the oldest church and the best Asian snack stalls, but also

Amsterdam's least salubrious area. This makes for a very diverse street scene: tourists, junkies, real old Amsterdamers, shoppers, Chinese residents, prostitutes and students go about their business between neon signs and canal-side houses, which seem much less smart here than on the upmarket Canal Ring. They were built between the 14th and the 16th century, when there were no strict building regulations, and as a result some have a wide, others a narrow frontage, some are tall and others low, some are imposing and others extremely crooked. It pays to stop for a while and look up at the façades above the shops or to take refuge from the hurrying crowds on Kalverstraat in the peace of the Begijnhof. Don't be shy about walking through narrow passages or taking a look in a little courtyard, as in this way you will discover hidden gems such as the restaurant Blauw aan de Wal or the book market behind the Oudemanhuispoort. The hubs of this richly varied activity are the squares Dam, Spui, Rembrandtplein and Nieuwmarkt.

1 AMSTERDAM DUNGEON
(120 B4) (*M* F4)

For those who like it macabre: an exhibition to send a shiver down your spine about the dark side of Amsterdam's history, including live demonstrations and a ghost train. *Daily 11am–5pm | admission 21 euros | Rokin 78 | www.the-dungeons.nl | tram 4, 9, 15, 16, 24 Rokin*

2 AMSTERDAM MUSEUM
(120 A–B4) (*M* F4)

A Baroque gate marks the entrance to the museum of city history, which has its home in a 17th-century former orphanage. Visitors first have access free of charge to the ● INSIDER TIP *Schuttersgalerij* with its 15 colossal paintings of members of the Amsterdam Civic Guard dating from the 17th century. Inside the museum too there is a lot to see: the

---

★ **Begijnhof**
Peace and quiet amid the bustle of the city → p. 30

★ **Nieuwe Kerk**
Towerless Gothic church on the Dam → p. 34

★ **Nieuwmarkt**
Lively square around the weighing house → p. 35

★ **Oude Kerk**
Amsterdam's oldest building → p. 36

★ **Canal Ring**
Unique historic ensemble of fine residences, bridges and canals → p. 38

★ **Anne Frank Huis**
The backyard hiding-place of the girl who wrote the famous diary → p. 40

★ **Westertoren**
Amsterdam's most popular church tower is commemorated in song → p. 44

★ **Rijksmuseum**
Masterpieces from Rembrandt to Vermeer → p. 50

★ **Van Gogh Museum**
The Sunflowers attract lots of visitors → p. 52

★ **Vondelpark**
Park with a fairground atmosphere → p. 52

MARCO POLO HIGHLIGHTS

collection, which occupies three floors, consists of no less than 40,000 items. In rooms 1 to 23, paintings, books, maps and models are employed to present the history of the city from the construction of the first dyke on the Amstel to the Golden Age and on to the era of squatters and coffee shops. A further highlight is the *Regentenkammer*, the meeting

Still-life with a beguine: in the Begijnhof

room for the directors of the orphanage, which is still entirely furnished in the style of the 17th century. At the entrance on St. Luciënsteeg a whole wall is clad with historic gable stones, which were once used by the people of Amsterdam to mark their addresses. *Mon–Fri 10am–5pm, Sat–Sun 11am–5pm | admission 10 euros (MK) | Kalverstraat 92 | www.amsterdammuseum.nl | tram 1, 2, 4, 5, 9, 14, 16, 24, 25 Spui or Rokin*

■ BEGIJNHOF ★ (120 A4) (*Ø F4*)

An oasis of peace and quiet in the buzzing city centre – at least, that is the case if you come on a weekday at a time when no busload of tourists throng the courtyard. White-painted houses are grouped around a small church and a few chestnut trees. Tiny front gardens are lovingly tended. The Begijnhof, the home of the beguines, was founded in 1346 at the edge of the city. It was a place of residence for single women who wished to live in a religious community but not become nuns. They mainly devoted themselves to caring for the aged. Two fires almost completely destroyed the Begijnhof in the 15th century, and the buildings as they are today largely date from the 17th century. House number 34, by contrast, was built in around 1470 and is thought to be the oldest wooden house in the Netherlands. Opposite the English Presbyterian chapel a 17th-century Catholic INSIDER TIP *secret church* is concealed in two residential buildings. About 100 people live in the Begijnhof to this day – but the last beguine died in 1971. *Daily 9am–5pm | entrances on Spui and Kalverstraat | tram 1, 2, 5 (Spui)*

■ BEURS VAN BERLAGE

(120 C2) (*Ø G3*)

A brick building on Damrak that looks like a castle, with a tall tower that can be

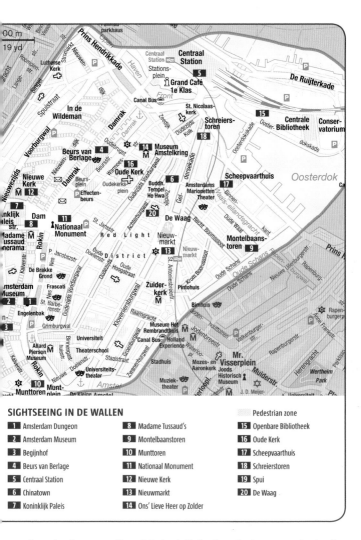

SIGHTSEEING IN DE WALLEN

1 Amsterdam Dungeon

2 Amsterdam Museum

3 Begijnhof

4 Beurs van Berlage

5 Centraal Station

6 Chinatown

7 Koninklijk Paleis

8 Madame Tussaud's

9 Montelbaanstoren

10 Munttoren

11 Nationaal Monument

12 Nieuwe Kerk

13 Nieuwmarkt

14 Ons' Lieve Heer op Zolder

15 Openbare Bibliotheek

16 Oude Kerk

17 Scheepvaarthuis

18 Schreierstoren

19 Spui

20 De Waag

Pedestrian zone

seen from afar: the commodity and stock exchange, built between 1897 and 1903 to plans by architect Hendrik Petrus Berlage, is regarded as one of the seminal works of modern architecture in the Netherlands thanks to its plain façade and openly visible method of construction.

Initially the clients were not at all pleased with the exchange: they would have preferred a prestigious-looking building in the neo-Renaissance style like the Rijksmuseum or the main station. However, architecture in a historical style was exactly what master builder Berlage wanted to get away from. He invited artist friends of his to decorate the building with contemporary ornamentation and works of art. Murals, sculptures, decorative ironwork and mottos complement the massive architecture and make the exchange building a complete work of art. Originally it housed no fewer than four exchanges: for goods, grain, maritime trade and stock. The imposing *Goods-exchange Hall* with its great glass roof, curved iron supports and two galleries is an exhibition space and concert hall today. *Accessible only for exhibitions and events | www.beursvanberlage.nl | tram 4, 9, 16, 24, 25 Dam*

5 CENTRAAL STATION (121 D1) (*ᗰ G3*)

The main station was built in 1889 in neo-Renaissance style by Petrus J. H. Cuypers, the architect of the Rijksmuseum. The impressive, 306-metre-long building stands on an artificial island and is flanked at the rear by the river IJ. This 'Travellers' Palace' is supported by more than 10,000 tree trunks that were rammed into the sandy ground. The decoration of the station is unusually sumptuous both inside and out, as it was intended to glorify the achievements of the industrial age while at the same time present a fine appearance, given its prominent position in the city. There is always a lot of coming and going on the square in front of the station – here you should be especially on your guard against pickpockets! From the rear side of the station, free ferries depart for Amsterdam-Noord. *Terminus for trams, buses, tourist and museum boats*

6 CHINATOWN (121 D2–3) (*ᗰ G3*)

Amsterdam's Chinatown is the district around Zeedijk and Nieuwmarkt. In the early 20th century many Chinese sailors came to the city. Some stayed and brought their families to join them. The Chinese still form a close-knit community and keep up their traditions. In Chinatown you will find authentic Chinese restaurants as well as Chinese bakeries, fashion boutiques and medical practices. The colourful icing on the cake is the ● Buddhist *Fo Guang Shan He Hua Temple(Tue–Sat noon–5pm, Sun 10am–5pm | Zeedijk 106–118 | Metro Nieuwmarkt),* which admits visitors without charge.

7 KONINKLIJK PALEIS ●
(120 B3) (*ᗰ F3*)

At first sight, the plain grey building on the Dam with its curtained windows

RELAX & ENJOY

Massages, beauty treatments, saunas – that's the ultimate relaxation, and the feeling of well-being is further enhanced if the surroundings are right – for example in the ● *Sauna Déco* **(120 A2) (*ᗰ F3*)** *(Mon, Wed–Sat noon–11pm, Tue 3–11pm, Sun 1–7pm | Herengracht 115 | tel. 020 6 23 82 15 | www.saunadeco.nl | tram 13, 14, 17*

Nieuwezijds Kolk) at the heart of the Canal Ring. The interior was brought here from a 1920s Paris department store that was demolished. With breaks to have a snack in the lounge, you can treat yourself to a hydro massage, steam bath, manicure or foot massage in a stylish and luxurious ambience.

A royal palace that once belonged to the citizens: when the Great Hall was built, it was part of the town hall

does not look like a royal palace. It is a tad disrespectfully known sometimes as 'Holland's biggest junk-room'. However, originally it was not built as a palace, but to serve as a town hall. Jacob van Campen was the architect of this building in the classical style, erected between 1648 and 1655. 13,659 piles had to be driven into the ground to support the weight of the imposing structure of Bentheim stone. A huge frieze depicting all kinds of sea monsters adorns the main façade. The most impressive features within are several monumental paintings by pupils of Rembrandt, the central hall and the furnishings in Empire style left behind from the French occupation in Napoleon's time. The city of Amsterdam did not make over its town hall to the monarchy until 1930. The main residence of the House of Orange is in The Hague – the king only stays in the Amsterdam palace for receptions, when it is not open to visitors. For up-to-date opening times,

see *www.paleisamsterdam.nl or tel. 020 6 20 40 60 | tram 1, 2, 4, 5, 9, 13, 14, 16, 17, 24, 25 Dam*

8 MADAME TUSSAUD'S

(120 B3) (*ØØ F3*)

If you always wanted to stand next to Rembrandt, Kylie Minogue or King Willem-Alexander and are prepared to pay a lot of money for the pleasure, here you can make your dreams come true among the wax figures of celebrities from all walks of life, some of them more real-looking than others. *Daily 10am– 5.30pm | admission 22 euros | Dam 20 | tram 4, 9, 14, 16, 24, 25 Dam*

9 MONTELBAANSTOREN

(121 E3–4) (*ØØ H4*)

At the corner of Waalseilandsgracht and Oudeschans, in what was once the ship-builders' district, this defensive tower was erected in the 16th century. As early as 1606 it lost its original purpose and was later fitted with a clock and chimes. Since 1878 Amsterdam's waterworks have used it to monitor the water level and the circulation in the canals. *Oudeschans 2 | Metro Nieuwmarkt*

⑩ MUNTTOREN (120 B5) (*ⓜ G4*)

The mint tower, built in 1620, stands at the confluence of the Singel and Amstel, and was originally part of the city defences. When the city of Dordrecht, which had the right to mint coins, was in danger of being occupied by French forces in 1672, gold and silver coins were minted here for a period. *Muntplein | tram 4, 9, 14, 16, 24, 25 Muntplein*

⑪ NATIONAAL MONUMENT (120 B3) (*ⓜ F3*)

The national monument *is on the* Dam, opposite the palace. This 22-metre obelisk, inaugurated in 1956, commemorates the victims of German occupation and is a monument to liberation and peace. In 1995 there was a bit of a scandal when it was found to be in need of restoration, and the only firm able to carry out the work turned out to be German. *Tram 4, 9, 14, 16, 24, 25 Dam*

⑫ NIEUWE KERK ★ (120 B3) (*ⓜ F3*)

The impressive Nieuwe Kerk on the Dam is Amsterdam's most famous church. It is not as new as the name suggests. Construction in the late Gothic style began in the 15th century, when the city had outgrown its first line of fortifications and the Oude Kerk had become too small. The church gained its present form after several fires and renovations in around 1540. Only 38 years later, during a campaign of iconoclasm, the Protestants removed every last statue and altar, meaning that the interior makes an extremely sober impression today. The main attraction in the church is the pulpit, adorned with elaborate carvings that took the sculp-

The obelisk of the Nationaal Monument on the Dam in remembrance of the German occupation

tor Albert Jansz Vinckenbrinck 15 years to complete.

The Nieuwe Kerk has no tower. Although foundations were laid for this purpose in 1565, political turbulence and iconoclastic fervour prevented construction. By the time things had quietened down, the city council was opposed to having a tower that would have been higher than the dome of the new town hall (today's palace). As a compromise the location of the town hall was shifted far enough back to permit at least the high transept of the church to adjoin the square.

Today the church is used as an exhibition space. Besides, the Nieuwe Kerk is still used for coronations of Dutch Kings and Queens such as the one in 2013 of King Willem-Alexander. It had already previously been used to celebrate his marriage in 2002 to the argentinian-born Máxima Zorreguieta. *Daily 10am–5pm | Dam | www.nieuwekerk.nl | tram 1, 2, 4, 5, 9, 13, 14, 16, 17, 24, 25 Dam*

13 NIEUWMARKT ★ (121 D3) (*ⓜ G4*)

Nieuwmarkt, a marketplace with many street cafés and musical cafés, as well as Asian snack bars, surrounds the old weighing house in the red-light district. It got its name in the 14th century, when part of Kloveniersburgwal was filled in to make the square. Originally it was a livestock market and place of execution. Today it is the site of occasional antique and book markets, and a food market is held there Mon–Sat. The size of the square means that on the outdoor terraces of the cafés it is still possible to catch the last rays of the sun there even shortly before sunset. *Metro Nieuwmarkt*

14 ONS' LIEVE HEER OP ZOLDER (120 C2) (*ⓜ G3*)

This little museum, which you can easily overlook from the outside, lies at the heart of the red-light district. On the lower floors it appears to be a perfectly normal 17th- century merchant's house. You can climb up and down the stairs to explore the nooks and crannies of this old canal house. The main attraction, however, is hidden away under the roof: a three-storey Catholic INSIDER TIP *secret church,* built in 1661 – fitted out with a high altar and two galleries. As the ruling Calvinists had prohibited Catholics from practising their religion openly, worshippers had to sneak into the house by a side entrance. *Mon–Sat 10am–5pm, Sun 1–5pm | admission 8 euros (MK) | Oudezijds Voorburgwal 40 | www.opsolder.nl | 10 min. on foot from the main station*

15 OPENBARE BIBLIOTHEEK ● (124 A5) (*ⓜ H3*)

Amsterdam's new municipal library is a real magnet for visitors. This impressive new building on Oosterdok island was opened in 2007 and is entirely furnished with the work of Dutch designers. On the

Books in a shrine to design:
Openbare Bibliotheek

upper floor there is a good self-service restaurant with a ☀ terrace, affording a wonderful view of the old quarter of Amsterdam. *Daily 10am–10pm | Oosterdokskade 143 | 5 min. on foot from the main station*

16 OUDE KERK ★ (120 C3) *(⌀ G3)*

Amsterdam's principal church, built around 1300 and today situated in the red-light district, is the oldest building in the city and was originally dedicated to St Nicholas, the patron saint of sailors. From the outside the Oude Kerk presents a rather motley appearance. This is because it was extended repeatedly over the course of time. As early as 1350 the narrow side aisles were widened, then the choir was enlarged, and later an ambulatory was built around the choir. In the 15th century several chapels were added, and in the 16th century the height of the nave and tower was increased. Despite the danger of fire, the structure was reinforced with wooden beams, as otherwise the sandy ground would not have been able to bear its weight. *Mon–Sat 11am–5pm, Sun 1–5pm | admission 5 euros (MK) | Oudekerksplein | www.oudekerk.nl | tram 4, 9, 16, 24, 25 Damrak*

17 SCHEEPVAARTHUIS (121 D–E3) *(⌀ H3)*

At first sight the 'house of seafaring' almost looks like the setting for a Batman film: forbidding, even a bit threatening. It stands on Binnenkade to the east of the main station. It was built in 1916 and is an early example of the brick Expressionism of the 1920s, which was to become famous as the style of the 'Amsterdam School', and is lavishly ornamented with maritime figures and decorative elements. Originally the seat of the most important shipping corporations, since 2007 it has been occupied by the *Grand Hotel Amrâth (p. 86)*. *Prins Hendrikkade 108–114 | 5 min. on foot from the main station*

18 SCHREIERSTOREN (121 D2) *(⌀ G3)*

From the battlements of the Schreierstoren, a semi-circular defensive tower dating from 1484, sailors' wives are supposed to have wept as their husbands' ships departed (the word 'schreier' suggests a person wailing). Although a 17th-century gable stone illustrates this story, it is untrue: originally the tower was called *schreyhoekstoren*, as it is the meeting point of two canals at an acute angle *(schreye hoek)*. In 1609 Henry Hudson sailed from this tower, which is depicted on many paintings, to North America, where he discovered Manhattan and founded New Amsterdam, the city later known as New York. The Hudson River and Hudson Bay are named after him. In the tower there is a INSIDER TIP cosy café. *Geldersekade | 5 min. on foot from the main station*

19 SPUI (120 A5) (*ℳ F4*)

Surrounded by nothing but old Amsterdam pubs such as *Café Luxembourg, Zwart* and INSIDER TIP *Café Hoppe*, which was established in 1670 and has a dimly lit wood-panelled interior with sand on the floor, Spui is regarded as the city's most traditional square. On Saturdays a *book market* takes place here. *Tram 1, 2, 5 Spui*

20 DE WAAG (121 D3) (*ℳ G4*)

Amsterdam's oldest secular building stands in the middle of Nieuwmarkt. It is the former weighing house, now home to an institute for new media and a café-restaurant. Built in 1488 as a city gate, in the 17th century, when the Canal Ring was constructed, it was converted into a weighing house. A number of craft guilds had their premises on the upper floors. Each guild even had its own entrance, as the different stones of the façade reveal to this day.

Beneath the roof of this building, the guild of surgeons installed a so-called *Anatomical Theatre*, which has been preserved completely intact. It can only be viewed during events held by the media institute. At one of the many public dissections that took place in the Anatomical Theatre, Rembrandt painted his famous Anatomy Lesson of Dr Tulp (1632), which today hangs in The Hague in the Het Mauritshuis museum. *Metro Nieuwmarkt*

The Oude Kerk has been extended repeatedly since 1300 – a choir here, a chapel there …

CANAL RING & JORDAAN

The completely preserved historic ensemble of the ★ *Canal Ring* is Amsterdam's biggest sight – quite literally.

The old canals, Singel, Herengracht, Keizersgracht and Prinsengracht, as well as countless smaller canals at right angles to these, form a semi-circle around the medieval city centre. In an area of some three square miles there are 160 canals and 600 bridges. The Canal Ring belongs to the UNESCO World Heritage Sites.

Around the year 1600 Amsterdam had become extremely wealthy through overseas trade. The beginning of the Golden Age was accompanied by a population boom: within a mere 50 years the number of residents increased fourfold. The old core of the city became too crowded and construction began on the Canal Ring, one of the most spectacular urban projects of the period. Its innovative features were not only the spacious layout of the canals, but also the fact that trees were planted on the banks. Criminals, vagrants and day labourers were brought in to do the digging. Rich merchants built their new residences and warehouses on the waterways, which originally served to drain the land. Building plots on the canals were expensive, however. As the purchase price and also later taxation were based on the width of the plot, most houses were built with a narrow frontage but continued a long way at the back. Herengracht, the 'canal of gentlemen', was named after the well-to-do merchants, Keizersgracht after Emperor ('Kaiser') Maximilian I, whose crown Amsterdam was permitted to include in its coat of arms, and Prinsengracht after the princes of the House of Orange. By 1680 the plan to extend the city had been carried out, and the Canal Ring was encircled by a defensive moat on the site of what is today Stadhouderskade.

The best way to visit the historic Canal Ring: by boat

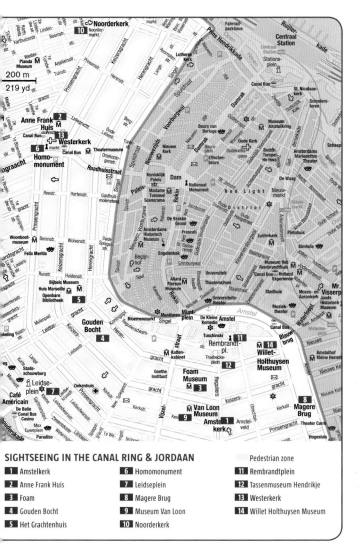

SIGHTSEEING IN THE CANAL RING & JORDAAN

1 Amstelkerk
2 Anne Frank Huis
3 Foam
4 Gouden Bocht
5 Het Grachtenhuis
6 Homomonument
7 Leidseplein
8 Magere Brug
9 Museum Van Loon
10 Noorderkerk

11 Rembrandtplein
12 Tassenmuseum Hendrikje
13 Westerkerk
14 Willet Holthuysen Museum

Pedestrian zone

Nowadays the Canal Ring with its grand old burghers' houses is still one of the best addresses in Amsterdam, even if many of these former dwellings are now home to legal practices and private banks. You can get a glimpse of luxurious interiors through the high curtainless windows of the old houses.

Jordaan, once a district for the poor, was built at about the same time as the Canal Ring. It is less upmarket but no less picturesque. Whole working-class families once had to live in damp basements in the quarter occupied today by many intellectuals and artists, ● galleries and design studios, where the atmosphere is almost that of a village. It was not until after the Second World War that conditions in Jordaan improved and the legendary neighbourhood spirit arose that is the subject of the sentimental songs that are still played in some of the 'brown cafés' in Amsterdam's most *gezellig* (friendly, cosy) district.

■1 AMSTELKERK (128 B1) (*♒ G5*)

The wooden Amstelkerk was built In 1669, when there was still a shortage of churches on the new Canal Ring. The place of worship constructed on the Amstelveld, a marshy area on Prinsengracht, was a plain white church without a tower that from outside looks a bit like a cowshed. The Amstelkerk is now also used for exhibitions and events. The adjoining building houses a chic restaurant with an attractive terrace, while on the open space in front of the church a INSIDER TIP flower market with prices not aimed at tourists is held on Monday mornings. *Amstelveld 12 | tram 4 Prinsengracht*

■2 ANNE FRANK HUIS ★
(123 D4) (*♒ F3*)

'Dear Kitty...': readers the world over recognise the words at the start of the entries in Anne Frank's diary. The spirited Jewish girl lived in hiding for two years during the Second World War with her family in this back-yard house on Prinsengracht – only to be deported after all at the last minute and in the end die from

AJAX

The Ajax Amsterdam football club (recognisable by white shirts with a red stripe) plays its home games in the Amsterdam Arena in the southeast of the city. The gigantic stadium looks like a spaceship that has landed on the grass. It has a retractable roof and holds almost 50,000 spectators. They need all those seats, as the Amsterdamers go crazy when Ajax play, and had plenty to shout about in 2012, when their team were the Dutch champions. Heroes of Dutch football like Johan Cruyff, Frank Rijkaard and Patrick Kluivert made Ajax famous. One thing that is surprising at first glance is that many fans wear the Israeli flag and paint a Star of David on their faces – as do some Tottenham Hotspurs supporters in London. It is said that Ajax was founded by Jews and remained a Jewish club for a long time, but this myth has little basis in fact: the fans' purpose is to distinguish themselves from the supporters of Feyenoord Rotterdam, who have right-wing tendencies.

You can get hold of tickets for Ajax games online, in the fan shop at the stadium or at Ticket Box sales outlets (usually kiosks and newsagents). You can also take part in a guided tour of the stadium *(daily every 45 minutes between 11am and 5pm | 12 euros). Amsterdam Arena (0) (♒ 0) (Arena Boulevard 1 | Metro 50, 54 (Strandvliet/ ArenA or Bijlmer) | www.ajax.nl | www.amsterdamarena.nl)*

the effects of imprisonment at Bergen-Belsen concentration camp.

Today the house is the headquarters of the Anne Frank Foundation and home to its museum. A secret door leads to the house at the back and the little flat in which the family was forced to live. The original diary is part of the impressive exhibition. The museum is always crowded with visitors so it is best to arrive early in the morning or late in the evening to avoid the queues. *Oct–Feb daily 9am–7pm, March–June, Sept daily 9am–9pm, July–Aug daily 9am–10pm | admission 8.50 euros | Prinsengracht 263 | www.annefrank.org | tram 13, 14, 17 Westermarkt*

3 FOAM (120 B6) (*U G5*)

In 2002 Amsterdam got its own museum of photography, housed in a canal house dating from the 19th century. Changing exhibitions about every aspect of photography can be seen here, from photojournalism to advertising photography and the works of Dutch photographic artists. *Sat–Wed 10am–6pm, Thu–Fri 10am–9pm | admission 8.75 euros (MK) | Keizersgracht 609 | www.foam.nl | tram 16, 24, 25 Keizersgracht*

4 GOUDEN BOCHT ●
(123 E6) (*U F–G 4–5*)

The section of Herengracht between Leidsestraat and Vijzelstraat is the 'golden arc', boasting houses that are noticeably larger and grander than most other buildings on the canals. They were built in the late 17th century by members of Amsterdam's new financial elite who wanted to distinguish themselves from the class of common merchants, and show off their wealth. For this reason many of them bought two plots of land at once; a fine residence was built at the front, with stables and accommodation for servants behind.

Anne Frank Huis: her moving diary was written here

The mayor of Amsterdam lived at house number 502. Number 518 can be seen from inside: it is the *Geelvinck Hinlopen* museum house *(Wed–Mon 11am–5pm | admission 8 euros | Herengracht (entrance from Keizersgracht 633) | tram 16, 24, 25 Vijzelstraat*

5 HET GRACHTENHUIS
(123 E6) (*U F4*)

The newest museum in a canal house in Amsterdam opened in 2011. In 1663 Philip Vingboons built this fine house for

German occupation. *Westermarkt | tram 13, 14 Westermarkt*

7 LEIDSEPLEIN (123 D6) (*E5*)

If you are looking for action, here it is: trams ring their bells, tourists pack the pubs, neon signs flash, street artists perform their tricks. At the heart of the city, Leidseplein is surrounded by cinemas, theatres, cafés and restaurants. It really throbs in the evenings, especially at weekends. *Tram 1, 2, 5, 6, 7, 10 Leidseplein*

8 MAGERE BRUG ● (128 C1) (*G5*)

Amsterdam's best-known bridge is particularly attractive after dark, when it is decked out with illuminations. The middle section of this white-painted wooden bridge can be raised to let ships through. *Kerkstraat/Amstel | tram 4 Prinsengracht | Metro Waterlooplein*

9 MUSEUM VAN LOON
(128 B1) (*G5*)

This magnificent canal house gives visitors an impression of how patrician families lived in Amsterdam in the 17th and 18th centuries. Built in 1671 for a wealthy merchant, the house was owned for a time by Rembrandt's pupil Ferdinand Bol. In 1884 it was bought by the Van Loon merchant family. The reception rooms, salons, dining rooms and bedrooms are open to visitors. The Baroque INSIDER TIP canal garden, which is visible from the small salon, is a relic of bygone days. *Wed–Mon 11am–5pm | admission 8 euros | Keizersgracht 672 | tram 16, 24, 25 Vijzelstraat*

10 NOORDERKERK (120 A1) (*F2*)

At its opening the Noorderkerk stood in the middle of a new housing area. Today it finds itself on Noordermarkt, one of Amsterdam's leafiest and most

Leidseplein is the bustling centre of the city

a patrician family; today, come and view an exhibition about the history of the Canal Ring, including historic plans and a model of the city. *Herengracht 386 | www.grachtenhuis.nl | tram 1, 2, 5 Koningsplein*

6 HOMOMONUMENT (123 D4) (*F3*)

Three rust-red marble slabs on the square in front of the Westerkerk were the world's first homosexual monument in 1987. It was placed there in memory of all persons who suffered persecution due to their homosexuality, first and foremost those who were victims of the

olde-worlde squares. At the rear, houses nestle up close to the church; not a single street approaches it at a right angle. Completed in 1623, the church is a typical Protestant place of worship with its central ground-plan focussing on the pulpit. *In summer open on Saturday morning | Noordermarkt | 10 min. on foot from the main station*

▇▇ REMBRANDTPLEIN (120 C6) *(ⅅ G4–5)*
In 1876 a statue of Rembrandt was erected on Botermarkt, which then gained a new name in honour of the painter. Now dominated by large-scale pubs and neon advertising, in the 1920s it was the rendezvous of the art scene. *Tram 4, 9, 14 Rembrandtplein*

▇▇ INSIDER TIP TASSENMUSEUM HENDRIKJE (120 C6) *(ⅅ G5)*
Another old canal-side house is the home to a museum devoted to the history of ladies' handbags from the 15th century to the present day. After admiring 4000 exhibits from the collection of Hendrikje Ivo, who gave her name to the museum, visitors can browse

Museum van Loon: see how a rich patrician family lived

in the museum shop, which sells bags by Dutch designers. *Daily 10am–5pm | Herengracht 573 | admission 9 euros | www.tassenmuseum.nl | tram 4, 9, 14 Rembrandtplein*

KEEP FIT!

Amsterdam's most attractive indoor swimming pool is right next to the Rijksmuseum: the ● *Zuiderbad* **(127 F2)** *(ⅅ F6)*. This brick building dates from 1897, when it was a school of cycling for Amsterdam ladies who wanted to practice staying upright on a penny-farthing. In 1912 it was converted to a swimming pool, and since then not a lot has changed at the Zuiderbad. Even the original changing cubicles have remained, and you can still enjoy the old Art Nouveau interior while swimming your lengths. It may not be a big pool, but you really can swim there undisturbed, as each morning on weekdays two lanes are reserved for swimmers doing lengths of the bath. It has little to attract children. *Mon 7am–12noon, Tue–Fri 7–9am, Sat 8am–3pm, Sun 10am–3.30pm | admission 3.40 euros | Hobbemastraat 26 | tram 2, 5 Hobbemastraat; 7, 10 Spiegelgracht* houses a glockenspiel with 49 bells. As it is the city's tallest tower, the superb view from the top rewards the effort of going up. *Mo–Sat 11am–3pm, glockenspiel Tue noon–1pm, tower ascent April–June Mon–Fri 10am–6pm, Sat 10am–8pm, Juli–Sept Mo–Sat 10am–8pm, Oct Mon–Fri 11am–5pm, Sat 10am–6pm | admission 7.50 euros | Prinsengracht 281/Westermarkt | tram 13, 14, 17 Westermarkt*

14 WILLET HOLTHUYSEN MUSEUM
(120 C6) (*M G5*)

This merchant's house of 1687 accommodates the art collection of Abraham Willet (1825–88). His wife's fortune enabled him to gather together an eclectic collection of art, crafts and fine furniture, which almost turned the home into a museum in his own lifetime. In 1889 his wife bequeathed the house including its collection to the city. The rooms are jammed full with ornate wall hangings, furniture, paintings and sculptures. *Mon–Fri 10am–5pm, Sat–Sun 11am–5pm | admission 8 euros | Herengracht 605 | www.willetholthuysen.nl | Metro Waterlooplein*

WATERLOO-PLEIN & PLANTAGE

Westertoren: from here you look down on the whole city

13 WESTERKERK (123 D4) (*M F3*)

On its completion in 1631 the Westerkerk, designed by Hendrick de Keyser, was the world's largest Protestant church. Inside it is a well-lit white hall church with restrained ornamentation in the Renaissance style. However, the ★ ☆ *Westertoren*, the 280-foot tower affectionately known as Oude Wester by the Amsterdamers, is more famous than the church itself. The tower is the landmark of the Jordaan quarter and has been celebrated in many songs. Its imperial-crown dome

Around Waterlooplein there is a district that doesn't really exist any more. It was once the Jewish quarter, and the majority of its inhabitants were deported and murdered during the Second World War. What remains are several synagogues, today home to the Jewish Museum, and some diamond-cutting shops and kosher restaurants. The appearance of the quarter has also changed since the days of the Jewish population. In the

1980s large-scale redevelopment was carried out here, leaving relatively little of the old building fabric intact.

Today a lot of students live between Nieuwe Herengracht and Oude Schans. They like to spend time on the daily flea market behind the Stopera and in the cafés of Jodenbreestraat.

Adjoining to the east is the more genteel and leafy residential district De Plantage. When the Canal Ring was laid out in the 17th century from west to east, it did not extend beyond the Amstel. Instead there were gardens and shipyards to the east. They made way only in the 19th century for an area of middle-class housing and a customs warehouse, the Entrepotdok. Today visitors come to this green district mainly for the Tropenmuseum, the zoo or the botanical garden. However, it is also worth taking a look at the Entrepotdok with its old warehouses, now converted into loft apartments.

■1■ BLAUWBRUG (121 D6) (*ﬄ G4*)
The sight of the Blauwbrug is a little bit reminiscent of the Pont Neuf in Paris. This elaborately decorated bridge across the Amstel was built in 1884. Its piers have the shape of the bows of ships, and the lanterns are crowned by golden imperial crowns. Despite the name, the bridge is not blue: a wooden predecessor on the same site was, however, once painted blue. *Amstelstraat/Amstel | tram 9, 14 | Metro Waterlooplein*

■2■ GASSAN DIAMONDS
(121 E4) (*ﬄ H4*)
Amsterdam was once an international centre of the diamond-cutting business. After the Second World War this business declined in importance, but there are still a few workshops where diamonds are cut and polished. Many of those that offer tours are purely visitor attractions, while the genuine workshops are not open to the public. Gassan Diamonds is the exception. In an imposing brick building dating from the late 19th century, 500 employees are engaged in polishing and selling these precious stones.

On the free tours, visitors can follow the stone's path from a raw diamond to a polished gem, and it goes without say-

JEWISH LIFE

From the 17th century onwards, the area around what is now called Waterlooplein was Amsterdam's Jewish quarter. Until the Second World War about 100,000 people lived here. In addition to the Ashkenazi, who were of German origin and mostly poor, it was home to Sephardic Jews from Portugal, who were traditionally wealthier, as well as a number of hapless Christians who were in financial difficulties. During the Second World War the Nazis brought the flourishing Jewish life of the district to an abrupt end. Before deportation to the concentration camps the Jews were forced to assemble in front of the Hollandse Schouwburg, a theatre situated in the middle of the quarter – today a place of commemoration.

The Nazis took away almost all Dutch Jews to the death camps, including 14-year-old Anne Frank, who is probably the most famous victim. Only 6000 Amsterdam Jews survived the war.

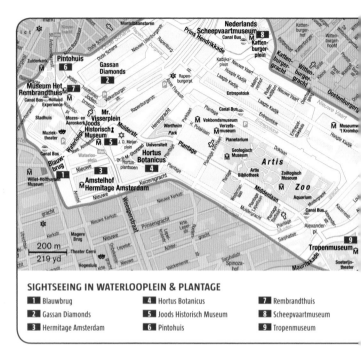

SIGHTSEEING IN WATERLOOPLEIN & PLANTAGE

1 Blauwbrug
2 Gassan Diamonds
3 Hermitage Amsterdam
4 Hortus Botanicus
5 Joods Historisch Museum
6 Pintohuis
7 Rembrandthuis
8 Scheepvaartmuseum
9 Tropenmuseum

ing that this is followed by a sales show. *Daily 9am–5pm | Nieuwe Uilenburger-straat 173–175 | free admission | www. gassan.com | Metro Waterlooplein*

3 HERMITAGE AMSTERDAM
(121 D6) (*ﬄ G5*)

Third foreign branch of the famous Russi-an art museum following that of London and Las Vegas. It is housed in a 17th-cen-tury former old people's home on the Amstel. Items from the huge collection of the mother institution, from ancient Greek jewellery to Rococo painting are on display. Worth seeing as well are the old church hall, the regency room and especially the INSIDER TIP fully furnished historical kitchen of the old people's home. *Daily 10am–5pm, Wed till 8pm | admission 15 euros | Nieuwe Herengracht*

14 | www.hermitage.nl | Metro Water-looplein

4 HORTUS BOTANICUS
(121 E–F 5–6) (*ﬄ H4*)

This is by no means your average botanical garden. It was here that more than 300 years ago Dutch doctors planted the first exotic herbs that domestic merchants and mariners brought back from their voyages to faraway places. This soon gave them a head start over their European colleagues in the field of tropical medicine. The old palm house is especially attractive, but don't fail to take a look at the futuristic new greenhouse too. In the *Hortuswinkel* flower bulbs and young shoots of rare plants are on sale. *Daily 10am–5pm | admission 8.50 euros | Plantage Middenlaan 2 | www.de-hortus.nl | tram 9, 14, 20 Mr. Visserplein*

5 JOODS HISTORISCH MUSEUM
(121 D5) (*ω H4*)

No fewer than four synagogues from the 17th and 18th centuries are home to the Jewish Historical Museum, which lies at the heart of what was once the Jewish quarter. As part of alterations to the museum in 1987 they were linked to each other by means of glass-roofed passages. The synagogue of the High German Jews, built in 1670, the *Grote Sjoel*, is the oldest but in spite of its name the smallest of the four places of worship. The others are the *Obbene, Dritt* and *Nieuwe Sjoel*. The exhibition presents the culture and religion of the Jewish community in the Netherlands, including of course the history of the persecution of Jews.

You can try kosher specialities in the museum café. *Daily 11am–5pm | admission 12 euros (MK) | Jonas Daniël Meijerplein 2–4 | www.jhm.nl | tram 9, 14 Mr. Visserplein | Metro Waterlooplein*

6 PINTOHUIS (121 D4) (*ω G4*)

The members of the Jewish-Portuguese Pinto family were bankers, the Rothschilds of the Golden Age. In about 1651 they bought this house opposite the Zuiderkerkhof. It was built in 1605 for a merchant of the VOC (Dutch East India Company), and was given the classical façade seen today in 1681. In the 20th century the building fell into decay but has now been restored and is used as a public library. In the entrance and the reading room the beautiful 17th-century murals and ceiling paintings can still be admired. *Sint Antoniesbreestraat 69 | Metro Nieuwmarkt*

7 REMBRANDTHUIS
(121 D4–5) (*ω G4*)

Rembrandt van Rijn (1606–69) is one of Amsterdam's most famous sons. Born in Leiden, the painter spent most of his life in the city of canals – not always in happy circumstances. His love life and his financial situation were subject to constant fluc-

The Hortus Botanicus is a refuge for peace and quiet in the middle of the city

A replica, but every bit as impressive as the original: the East Indies ship *Amsterdam*

tuation. In 1639 he bought this house in what was then the Jewish quarter. Money problems forced him to sell it in 1660 and move to rented accommodation.

Back in 1908 the house in Joden-breestraat was restored and converted to a museum, then given an extension in 1999. It is now home to the world's biggest collection of etchings, copper-plate engravings and drawings by Rembrandt. The old part of the house has been furnished as it might have looked in Rembrandt's time, including his studio. *Daily 10am–5pm | admission 10 euros (MK) | Jodenbreestraat 4–6 | www.rembrandthuis.nl | tram 9, 14 (Mr. Visserplein), Metro | Waterlooplein*

8 SCHEEPVAARTMUSEUM
(124 B5) (*Ø J4*)

The maritime museum, housed in what was once a naval arsenal dating from the 17th century has a large collection of ships' models, old navigation instruments, weapons, charts and paintings that illustrate the glorious history of Dutch seafaring. It was reopened in 2011 following comprehensive renovations and now has three multimedia themed exhibitions about whaling, the Golden Age and the port of Amsterdam today. Seven further rooms are devoted to exhibits such as models of yachts and marine charts which appeal to those interested in maritime matters.

Next to the museum is a replica of the INSIDER TIP East Indies ship Amsterdam. Tickets for the museum include a visit to the ship, which provides a good impression of how sailors lived in the 18th century. The crew scurry round all day, busy unloading the cargo, scrubbing the deck and singing sea shanties. The original Amsterdam didn't sail all the seven seas, but sank in a storm off the English coast on its maiden voyage. *Daily 9am–5pm |*

admission 15 euros (MK) | Kattenburger-
plein 1 | www.scheepvaartmuseum.nl |
bus 22, 32 Kattenburgerplein

🔟 TROPENMUSEUM ●
(129 E1) (*ØØ J5*)

The life and culture of tropical and sub-
tropical regions are the theme of this
museum. It was founded in 1910 as a
colonial museum, and displayed items
brought back by the Dutch from their
colonies in Southeast Asia and South
America. Nowadays the Tropenmuseum
has an extremely diverse collection of
objects from a wide range of countries,
which are presented grouped by region
with the assistance of up-to-date multimedia technology. The highlights include
reconstructions of streets from far-away
countries, for example a slum in Manila.
Tue–Sun 10am–5pm | admission 12 eu-
ros | Linnaeusstraat 2 | www.tropenmu-
seum.nl | tram 6, 9, 14 Mauritskade

OUD ZUID & DE PIJP

**To the southwest of Museumplein lies
the upper middle-class district named
Oud Zuid. Built in the 19th century, the
houses here are more imposing, the
streets wider and the green spaces more
extensive than in other parts of the city.**
At the northwestern edge of Oud Zuid
(the 'Old South') you will find Vondelpark, Amsterdam's 'green lung', which
was donated by rich citizens. Today
Oud Zuid remains one of Amsterdam's
most exclusive districts. Property prices
are higher only on the Canal Ring. It is
also an area for shops with high-class
designer fashion, expensive restaurants
and the city's best museums. To the east
is INSIDERTIP De Pijp, which was built as

a quarter for workers in the same period.
What was once considered poor is seen
by many as picturesque today, and this is
one of the most vibrant and multicultural
parts of Amsterdam.

1️⃣1️⃣ HEINEKEN EXPERIENCE
(128 B2) (*ØØ F6*)

Beer is no longer produced in the
135-year-old Heineken brewery on Stadhouderskade, but visitors can take an in-
teractive journey through the process of
brewing and design their own Heineken

LOW BUDGET

▶ Every Wednesday at 12.30pm in
the *Concertgebouw* **(127 E3)** (*ØØ E6*)
(Concertgebouwplein 2–6 | www.
concertgebouw.nl | tram 3, 5, 12, 16
Concertgebouw) there is a half-hour
lunch concert with free admission.

▶ Climb up the stepped roof
of the Nemo Science Center
(121 F2) (*ØØ H3*) (Oosterdok 2 |
10 min. on foot from the main station) to get a fantastic panoramic view
of the old quarter of Amsterdam
without paying a penny. In summer
you can sit around in comfort on the
beanbags of the café.

▶ For cut-price admission tickets
to various sights of the city, go
to a small, nameless shop at the
corner of *Damrak* and *Zoutsteeg*
(120 B3) (*ØØ G3*). The only drawback
is that the tickets are not valid during the most popular visiting hours.
If you can live with that, then the
saving at Madame Tussaud's, for
instance, is up to 10 euros.

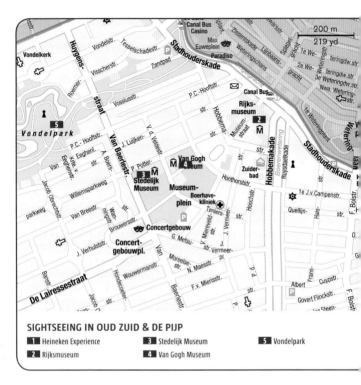

SIGHTSEEING IN OUD ZUID & DE PIJP

1 Heineken Experience   **3** Stedelijk Museum   **5** Vondelpark
2 Rijksmuseum   **4** Van Gogh Museum

bottle. And it goes without saying that there's no need to leave feeling thirsty: a tasting forms an essential part of your Heineken experience. *Daily 11am–7pm | admission 18 euros | Stadhouderskade 78 | tram 16, 24, 25 Heinekenplein*

2 RIJKSMUSEUM ★ (127 F2) (*𝄞 F5*) It's impossible to overlook the Rijksmuseum on Museumplein. This venerable treasure-house of art and history, designed by the architect Petrus J. H. Cuypers in a hybrid style of Gothic Revival and Renaissance, opened to the public in 1885. Alongside one of the most important collections of paintings in the Netherlands, it has vast holdings of historic artefacts and examples of crafts.

After more than ten years of renovations the museum was reopened in 2013. Since then the entrance is located in the new atrium, that is accessible from the tunnel under the building. Additionally, a new smaller building was constructed for Asian works of art. However, the bulk of the 375 Mio. euros building budget was invested in restoring the library and the hallways, that now shine in their former splendour. The main focus of the collection is placed on the Dutch Golden Age. Among the paintings of course is Rembrandt's 'Company of Captain Frans Banning Cocq', better known as 'The Nightwatch'. In 1642 Rembrandt's customers were not satisfied with the way he carried out their commission, but today millions of visitors from all over the world come every year to see this painting close up. The exhibition also presents works by other Dutch painters such as Frans Hals, Jan Steen, Jacob van Ruisdael and Jan Vermeer. There is always a crowd in front of Vermeer's Kitchen Maid (1660) and Woman in Blue Reading a Letter (1662–64). Genre scenes such as this give an astonishingly immediate glimpse of life in middle-class Dutch households of the 17th century – as do Jan Steen's Morning Toilet (1663) and Pieter de Hooch's Larder dating from 1660. *Daily 9am–6pm | admission 10 euros (MK), free for under 18s | Stadhouderskade 42 | www.rijksmuseum. nl | tram 2, 5 Hobbemastraat*

■ STEDELIJK MUSEUM
(127 E2) (*ᗝ E6*)

The Stedelijk Museum holds one of the most significant collections of modern and contemporary art of the Netherlands. It was reopened in 2012 after years of renovations and extension work. Since then, a bath-like-shaped futuristic construction is attached to the back of the 19th century building designed by the Amsterdam architect office Benthem Crouwel. The annexe, whose front is wainscotted with seemless panels of a composite material only so far seen in aeroplane and ship building, contains the foyer and two big halls for temporary exhibitions. The collection can still be seen in the old building and encompasses the most important modern works of art from Claude Monet to Mondrian right up to Karel Appel and Bruce Nauman. *Daily 10am–6pm, Thu until 10pm | admission 10 euros (MK) | Paulus Potterstraat 13 | www.ste delijk.nl | tram 1, 2, 3, 5, 7, 10, 12, 14 Van Baerlestraat*

Even its exterior is a magnet in the Museumplein: the Rijksmuseum

The modern pavilion of the Van Gogh Museum is devoted to changing exhibitions

■4 VAN GOGH MUSEUM ★
(127 E–F2) (*ID E6*)

The state-run Van Gogh Museum possesses the world's largest collection of works by the artist to whom it is dedicated. This is possible due to the otherwise regrettable fact that during his lifetime almost no paintings by Vincent van Gogh (1853–1890) found a buyer: they stayed in the family, which bequeathed the 205 paintings and 500 drawings to the museum in 1963. The exhibition traces the eventful and tragic life of the artist from his early years in the Netherlands and his time in Paris and the south of France to his death in Auvers-sur-Oise. Apart from self-portraits and a version of the Sunflowers the highlights of the collection include The Potato Eaters, The Yellow House, The Bedroom and Wheatfield with Crows.

The museum was built in 1973 by Gerrit Rietveld; in 1999, a three-storey pavilion was built next to it and connected to the older part of the museum by an underground passage in order to hold changing exhibitions of art from Van Gogh's time. *Daily 10am–6pm, Fri until 10pm | admission 15 euros (MK) | Paulus Potterstraat 7 | www.vangoghmuseum.nl | tram 1, 2, 3, 5, 7, 10, 12, 14 Van Baerlestraat*

■5 VONDELPARK ★ ●
(126–127 C–E 2–3) (*ID C–E 5–6*)

On summer afternoons you can hardly see the park for the people. Vondelpark is less a green space than a meeting place, bicycle route, event venue and playground for the people of Amsterdam. Back in the 1960s it was a magnet for hippies from all over the world who settled there permanently until the police put an end to their occupation of the park in 1975. Its origins were much more conventional. The 120-acre space,

stages where INSIDER TIP open-air performances are held in summer. The *Vertigo* café has one of the most attractive and lively terraces in the city, and there are alternatives in the *Melkhuis* restaurant and the *Blue Teahouse. Tram 1, 2, 3, 5, 7, 10, 12, 14 Van Baerlestraat*

MORE SIGHTS

EYE FILM INSTITUTE (124 A2) (*Ø G2*)

It would be hard not to notice the futuristic white architecture of the *Eye Film Institute*, which has stood on the north bank of the IJ behind the main station since 2011. It was designed by the Austrian architectural practice of Delugan Meissl, who gained renown with the Porsche Museum in Stuttgart. Behind its sculptural façade lies the Dutch film museum with four cinema screens, 1200 square metres of exhibition space, a museum shop and a waterfront café. In the Filmlab you can click your way through an interactive version of the museum's collection. It's worth doing the five-minute ⚄ crossing on the ferry to watch a film or see an exhibition, or just to have a cup of coffee and watch what's happening on the water. *Daily 10am–10pm | IJprom-*

named after the Renaissance poet Joost van den Vondel, was the first public park in Amsterdam when it was laid out in 1877. Well-off citizens had got together to create an oasis of greenery for their district of new residences south of the Canal Ring. Vondelpark is home to three

IMMIGRANTS IN THE PARK

When you walk through Vondelpark in summer, you hear them squawking; in winter, when the branches of the trees are bare, you can see them clearly too: bright green parakeets. To be precise, they are ring-necked parakeets, a kind of Asian parrot that is commonly kept as a pet in Europe. In 1976 an owner released his pair in Vondelpark because they made too much noise. It didn't take

the birds long to breed, and in Vondelpark there are several trees suitable for roosting at night. At sundown hundreds of parakeets gather there every day and stage a deafening, cacophonous concert. The local residents are none too keen on them, and neither are the Dutch animal protection authorities, as these immigrants compete with native birds for places to breed and supplies of food.

enade 1 | www.eyefilm.nl | free ferry to
Buiksloterweg from the north side of the
main station

IJBURG (131 D4) *(∅ 0)*

In the east of Amsterdam a new archi-
pelago is arising in the IJsselmeer. Seven
artificial islands are being created to
form the new district of IJburg, where it
is planned that 45,000 people will one
day live and work. Fans of modern architecture will find plenty to interest them
here. Especially on the *Steigereiland,* the
island nearest to the city, there are lots of
curiosities, from a quarter with floating
houses to terraced houses in a colourful
mix of styles. In summer the appealing
improvised ● city beach of *Blijburg aan
Zee* attracts many residents from the inner city to the eastern end of the new
archipelago. *Closed Mon | Muiderlaan
1001 | tram 26 to the last stop (IJburg),
then 5 minutes walk along Pampuslaan |
www.blijburg.nl*

INSIDER TIP NIEUWENDAM ●

(125 D–F 1–2) *(∅ M–N1)*

If you want to get away from the noise
and crowds of the city and see Dutch village life without taking a long journey,
look no further than Nieuwendammerdijk. In what used to be a dyke village on
the north side of the river IJ one quaint
little house stands next to another – all
protected as historic buildings. In summer it's pleasant to sit outside the small
café by the harbour. *Bus 32 from Centraal
Station Merelstraat*

INSIDER TIP HET SCHIP (122 C1) *(∅ E1)*

This residential block, which Michel de
Klerk designed in 1919, took its name
from its shape, and it does look like a
ship. Het Schip is a fine example of the
brick-built Expressionist style: unusual
ornamentation and window forms and

pretty though non-functional turrets
adorn this social housing. Within the
curving block you can visit a post office
designed by De Klerk in the 1920s and a
flat that has been made into a museum.
*Tue–Sun 11am–5pm | admission 7.50 eu-
ros (MK) | Spaarndammerplantsoen 140 |
bus 22 Spaarndammerplantsoen*

AROUND
AMSTERDAM

MARKEN (131 D3) *(∅ 0)*

With its green wooden houses this village, which has been situated on an
island in the IJsselmeer since the St
Julian's Day flood of 1164, is a piece of
picture-postcard Holland. The little old
houses snuggle together by the quayside, sailing boats bob up and down in
the harbour, and some old ladies still

Swap the city for the beach? Zandvoort is no more than half an hour from Amsterdam by train

wear traditional costume. In one of the harbour cafés you can drink coffee with a view of the IJsselmeer or take a walk to the lighthouse. For a nice atmosphere, guaranteed to be without coach loads of tourists, go to the little INSIDER TIP Hof van Marken hotel restaurant in the village centre *(Buurt II no. 15 | tel. 0299 60 13 00 | www.hofvanmarken.nl). Bus 311 goes every 30 min. from the main station to Marken, journey time approx. 40 min. | return trip with Waterlanddag-Kaart (buy it from the driver) 10 euros*

If you feel like cycling there, you can get to Marken within two hours on a pleasant bike tour. Behind the main station take the ferry to IJplein, ride along Meeuwenlaan, turn right onto Nieuwendammerdijk, then stay on the dyke by the IJsselmeer. After the village of Uitdam turn right again and pedal to Marken on the connecting dyke. The distance is about 22 km.

ZANDVOORT (130 A4) (*∅ 0*)

It takes barely half an hour by train to get from the main station to Zandvoort aan Zee, the North Sea resort on Amsterdam's doorstep. With its high-rises and faceless apartment blocks, this is not an attractive little place, but to make up for that there is a long, long sandy beach, and you only need to walk along it a short way to leave the town behind.

On warm summer weekends it can be extremely crowded here, but outside the peak season you will have the gulls and hardly anyone else for company. Typical features of Zandvoort are the fishing carts that tractors pull across the beach. They sell all sorts of deep-fried food and INSIDER TIP delicious prawn rolls. *Trains to Zandvoort every 30 min. from the main station, in winter change at Haarlem | return ticket 10.20 euros*

FOOD & DRINK

Cambodian, Ethiopian, Peruvian or Surinamese – if you are willing to experiment, you can eat your way around the world in Amsterdam.

And that's a good thing, some gourmets say, as Dutch food doesn't have a great reputation. The Calvinist tradition regarded all culinary pleasure as unnecessary, even sinful, and for centuries the people of Holland preferred to eat what was plain and nourishing. For example *stamppot:* mashed potato mixed with pieces of sausage or meat and cabbage. In recent years Dutch cooking has made progress. Chefs in good restaurants are inventing modern variations on local and seasonal specialities, rediscovering forgotten vegetables and experimenting with influences from all over the globe. Dutch asparagus is excellent, and a bite of tender *hollandse nieuwe haring* can be relied on to convert those who were averse to matjes herring before.

Specialities from the former Dutch colonies also have an established place in the national cuisine. In Amsterdam all the children know what *nasi goreng* (rice with shrimps and chicken) or *saté* (skewered chicken with peanut sauce) is. The city's Indonesian restaurants are among the best in Europe. And in Chinatown you have opportunities to try authentic Chinese food that doesn't make compromises to please European palates.

There is a huge range of places to eat, with a snack bar or restaurant on almost every corner. Prices are relatively high

Photo: Moeders restaurant

Pancakes, Peking duck and *bami goreng*: Amsterdam's gastronomic scene is as multicultural as its people

and service is often not all it could be. If you are keeping the costs down, the cosy, typically Dutch *eetcafés,* where for the most part Dutch food with a Mediterranean touch is dished up, are a good bet. The more upmarket *grand cafés* have either a modern or a old-world coffeehouse atmosphere, and serve cakes and light meals all day. Normal *cafés* have the character of pubs. Asian snack bars, of which there are many in Chinatown, will give you a cheap and tasty meal but are not places to linger.

The most popular drink is still a *biertje,* beer served in a small glass. Along with local brews like Amstel or Brandt, the sweeter Belgian beers are popular. In summer try *witbier*, a pale beer served with a slice of lemon. Don't fail to taste some *genever* – a spirit related to gin and made with juniper berries. The older it is, the spicier the taste.

At lunchtime the options in Amsterdam are limited if you want more than a sandwich or soup, as the Dutch take their main meal in the evening – traditionally

Long-established:
Café Américain

as early as 6pm, now often later. Most restaurants don't open at midday, and many *eetcafés* close at 9.30pm.

EETCAFÉS

DE BAKKERSWINKEL ⓒ (122 C2) (*ØD E1*)

In a building that once belonged to the Westergasfabriek gasworks, the small Bakkerswinkel chain has opened a branch that has delicious salads and sandwiches, using organic ingredients from the Amsterdam region where possible. *Closed Mon | Polonceaukade 1–2 | tel. 020 6 88 06 32 | tram 10 Van Hallstraat*

CAFÉ AMSTERDAM (122 C2) (*ØD D2*)

The former pump house of the waterworks makes for an impressive setting. Hearty sandwiches at midday, steak and fries in the evening. *Daily | Watertorenplein 6 | tel. 020 6 82 26 66 | tram 10 (van Hallstraat)*

MORLANG (123 E6) (*ØD F4*)

Creative international cuisine and a young clientele in a wonderful canalside house. The surroundings upstairs are more pleasant than in the basement. *Daily | Keizersgracht 451 | tel. 020 6 25 26 81 | tram 1, 2, 5 Keizersgracht*

PIET DE LEEUW (128 B2) (*ØD F5*)

The very first *eetcafé* in Amsterdam. Famous for steaks and enormous portions of plaice that don't fit on the plate. *Daily | Noorderstraat 11 | tel. 020 6 23 71 81 | tram 4, 9, 14 Rembrandtplein*

SPANJER & VAN TWIST (123 E4) (*ØD F3*)

A pretty café with a well-loved little terrace on Leliegracht. Light midday and evening meals, tasty snacks to go with the beer. *Daily | Leliegracht 60 | tel. 020 6 39 01 09 | tram 13, 14, 17 Westerkerk*

VILLA ZEEZICHT ★ (120 A2) (*ØD F3*)

A small café with outdoor seating in summer on the bridge over the Singel canal.

Excellent filled rolls (*broodjes),* divine *appeltaart* with cinnamon ice cream. *Daily | Torensteeg 7 | tel. 020 6 26 74 33 | tram 1, 2, 5, 13, 14, 17 Dam*

GRAND CAFÉS

CAFÉ AMÉRICAIN ★ (123 D6) (*ILL E5*)
Elegant Art Nouveau café in the hotel of the same name. *Daily | Leidseplein 97 | tel. 020 5 56 30 09 | tram 1, 2, 5, 7, 10 Leidseplein*

GRAND CAFÉ 1E KLAS
(121 D1) (*ILL G3*)
Station cafés are not often inviting places, but this one is an exception, serving hamburgers and apple cake in historic fin-de-siècle surroundings. *Daily | Stationsplein 15 |platform 2b in the main station | tel. 202 6 25 01 31 | tram all routes Centraal Station*

DE JAREN (120 B5) (*ILL G4*)
A large café with a restaurant upstairs. Good, plain food. In summer reserve a table on the 🌿 terrace, where you get a wonderful view of the city. *Daily | Nieuwe Doelenstraat 20–22 | tel. 020 6 25 57 71 | tram 4, 9, 16, 24, 25 Muntplein*

STANISLAVSKI (127 F1) (*ILL E5*)
Previously the foyer of the Stadsschouwburg theatre, now a chic grand café with lounge atmosphere. *Daily | Leidseplein 26 | tel. 020 7 95 99 95 | tram 1, 2, 5, 7, 10 Leidseplein*

RESTAURANTS: EXPENSIVE

INSIDER TIP BLAUW AAN DE WAL
(120 C3) (*ILL G3*)
In the middle of the red-light district a narrow alley leads to this culinary oasis. The courtyard was once part of a monastery. Outstanding French food and good service. *Closed Sun–Mon | Oudezijds Achterburgwal 99 | tel. 020 3 30 22 57 | Metro Nieuwmark*

ENVY (123 D5) (*ILL E–F4*)
Hip restaurant with a stylish modern design in a narrow room on Prinsen-

---

★ **Villa Zeezicht**
Wonderful *appeltaart* above the canal in a relaxed atmosphere → p. 58

★ **Café Américain**
Grand café in elegant Art Deco style → p. 59

★ **Greetje**
Pleasure of a rare kind: modern Dutch kitchen – from dune vegetables to blood sausage → p. 60

★ **Hoi Tin**
A wide choice of dishes in Chinatown → p. 63

★ **Moeders**
Traditional Dutch fare the way 'moeder' makes it → p. 64

★ **Morita-Ya**
Affordable Japanese food → p. 64

★ **Pata Negra**
The tapas taste as they do in Spain – with the atmosphere of Seville thrown in → p. 64

★ **Tujuh Maret**
Authentic Indonesian cooking → p. 65

MARCO POLO HIGHLIGHTS

LOCAL SPECIALITIES

▶ **appeltaart** – apple tart, cold or warm, served with slagroom (whipped cream)

▶ **ba pao** – steamed Chinese rolls filled with meat or vegetables

▶ **bitterballen** – deep-fried meatballs in breadcrumbs

▶ **erwtensoep** – thick pea soup with bits of sausage, accompanied by rye bread and bacon

▶ **hollandse nieuwe** – young matjes herring

▶ **kipsaté** – Indonesian skewered chicken with peanut sauce

▶ **koffie verkeerd** – ('coffee the wrong way round') milky coffee

▶ **kroket** – deep-fried meat or shrimp croquettes

▶ **loempia** – spring roll with or without meat

▶ **mosselen** – mussels cooked in white wine, served with fries and mayonnaise

▶ **nasi/bami goreng** – rice or noodles with shrimps and chicken (Indonesian speciality)

▶ **oliebollen** – sweet dough with raisins fried in oil

▶ **ontbijtkoek** – breakfast confectionery with honey, ginger, cinnamon and cloves

▶ **ossenworst** – raw beef sausage, originally a Jewish speciality

▶ **pannekoeken** – egg pancakes (photo left)

▶ **patat oorlog** – French fries with mayonnaise, peanut sauce and onions

▶ **poffertjes** – mini-pancakes with icing sugar

▶ **roti** – Indian or Surinamese flat bread filled with meat or vegetables

▶ **stamppot** – mashed potato with pieces of sausage or meat and vegetables

▶ **uitsmijter** – slices of bread with boiled ham, cheese and fried eggs (photo right)

▶ **vla** – a thick vanilla pudding

gracht. All guests sit at a long counter to eat lots of delicious tidbits and drink a good vintage from the really extensive wine list. *Daily | Prinsengracht 381 | tel. 020 3 44 64 07 | tram 13, 14, 17 Westermarkt*

GREETJE ★ (121 E4) (*ⓜ H4*)
Restaurant with a relaxed atmosphere, hidden away in a side street. The style of cooking is truly unusual: modern Dutch cuisine, from baked black pudding to halibut with dune vegetables and crème

brûlée with liquorice root. *Closed Mon | Peperstraat 23 | tel. 020 779 74 50 | Metro Nieuwmarkt*

HOTEL DE GOUDFAZANT (125 D2) *(∭ K2)*
Trendy restaurant in an industrial district in Noord. French-influenced Dutch dishes are served beneath a huge chandelier in an unadorned warehouse atmosphere. *Closed Mon | Aambeeldstraat 10h | tel. 020 636 51 70 | bus 38 Hamerstraat*

INSIDER TIP DE KAS 😊 (0) *(∭ K7)*
Organic vegetables from the restaurant's own garden in an 8-metre-high greenhouse. The latest in Dutch food, and an out-of-the-ordinary atmosphere. Book ahead if you want to come in the evening! *Closed Sun | Kamerlingh Onneslaan 3 | tel. 020 4 62 45 62 | tram 9 Hoogweg*

MAMOUCHE (128 B2) *(∭ F6)*
High-class Moroccan eatery in De Pijp. Guests help themselves to tea from a cauldron bubbling in the middle of the restaurant. Wonderful *tajine* (braised lamb with nuts, dried fruit, olives and coriander). *Quellijnstraat 104 | tel. 020 673 63 61 | www.restaurantmamouche.nl | tram 16, 24, 25 Albert Cuypmarkt*

DE OESTERBAR (127 F1) *(∭ E5)*
Long-established fish restaurant on Leidseplein with a wide choice ranging from Zeeland oysters to lobster and veal sweetbread. *Daily | Leidseplein 10 | tel. 020 6 23 29 88 | tram 1, 2, 5, 7, 10 Leidseplein*

PONT 13 (0) *(∭ 0)*
A converted IJ ferry, now a bit off the beaten track in the timber dock. Terrific atmosphere, and really good food. The fish soup with rouille is excellent. *Haparandadam 50 | tel. 020 770 27 22 | www.pont13.nl | bus 48 Oostzaanstraat*

SEGUGIO (128 B1) *(∭ G5)*
Classy Italian with minimalist styling. The dried cod and risotto with white truffles are classics here, and the pasta is made fresh every day. Book well ahead! *Closed Sun | Utrechtsestraat 96a | tel. 020 3 30 15 03 | tram 4 Prinsengracht*

Organic food in a greenhouse: De Kas

DE SILVEREN SPIEGEL (120 B1) *(∭ G3)*
Atmospheric restaurant in a crooked old house dating from 1614. The emphasis is on regional products and contemporary interpretations of Dutch dishes. *Closed Sun | Kattengat 4/6 | tel. 020 6 24 65 89 | tram 1, 2, 5, 13, 17 Nieuwezijds Kolk*

VAN VLAANDEREN (128 B2) *(∭ G6)*
French cuisine that has earned its star in an intimate, friendly atmosphere. *Closed Sun–Mon | Weteringschans*

175 | tel. 020 6 22 82 92 | tram 1, 2, 5 Spui

D'VIJFF VLIEGHEN (120 A4) *(🕮 F4)*
Wooden genever barrels, Rembrandt etchings and a collection of old weapons create an authentic mood in these five 17th-century houses. The menu too upholds Dutch traditions. *Daily | Spuistraat 294–302 | tel. 020 5 30 40 60 | tram 1, 2, 5 Spui*

YAMAZOTO (128 B4) *(🕮 F7)*
It's all there in the restaurant of the Japanese Okura Hotel, including waitresses in kimonos and a fish pond. The sashimi is served on ice, the beef raw with a hot griddle. *Daily | Ferdinand Bolstraat 333 | tel. 020 6 78 83 51 | tram 25 Cornelis Troostplein*

RESTAURANTS: MODERATE

BALTHAZAR'S KEUKEN (123 D5) *(🕮 E4)*
Small restaurant with an intimate atmosphere. Choose between French-influenced fish and meat menus for around 28 euros. Opens only three nights a week. *Closed Sat–Tue | Elandsgracht 108 | tel. 020 4 20 21 14 | tram 7, 10 Elandsgracht*

CAFÉ DE PONT ☼ **(124 A3)** *(🕮 H2)*
This simple and likeable restaurant is right next to the quay for the IJ ferry. In summer you can sit outside with a nice view across the water. Changing daily menu, good tapas at a reasonable price. *Daily | Buiksloterweg 3–5 | tel. 020 6 36 33 88 | Ferry Buiksloterwegveer (leaves behind the station)*

GOURMET RESTAURANTS

Beddington's (128 B2) *(🕮 G5)*
In a little side street off Utrechtsestraat Jean Beddington works in her open kitchen to conjure up unusual delights for her guests. How about black pudding with scallops and cauliflower pannacotta? *Menu 55 euros | closed Sun–Mon | Utrechtsedwarsstraat 141 | tel. 020 6 20 73 93 | tram 4 Prinsengracht*

Breitner (128 C1) *(🕮 G5)*
This restaurant with a stylish design and a lovely view of the Magere Brug lies directly on the Amstel. The house speciality is fried duck liver with pear chutney. The recommended wines are renowned. *Menu approx. 50 euros | closed Sun | Amstel 212 | tel. 020 6 27 78 79 | Metro Waterlooplein*

Christophe (123 E4) *(🕮 F3)*
French cuisine with an Arabian touch by a Michelin-starred chef and perfect service are the strengths of Christophe. The soberly furnished restaurant lies on one of Amsterdam's loveliest canals. *Menu approx. 70 euros | closed Sun–Mon | Leliegracht 46 | tel. 020 6 25 08 07 | tram 13, 14, 17 Westermarkt*

Halvemaan (0) *(🕮 0)*
Experimental cuisine is the reason to go out to the suburb of Buitenveldert: duck sausage with date puree or beef tartare with oysters are examples of the combinations at Halvemaan. In summer the terrace by the pond is a great place to sit. *Menu approx. 70 euros | closed Sat–Sun | Van Leijenberghlaan 320 | tel. 020 6 44 03 48 | Metro Zuid W.T.C.*

CASA PERÚ (123 D2) *(⊅ F4)*

Peruvian restaurant run by a friendly Andean family. *Ceviche* – raw fish marinated in lemon juice – is delicious and always fresh here. *Daily | Leidsegracht 68 | tel. 020 6 20 37 49 | tram 7, 10 Raamplein*

FIFTEEN (124 C4) *(⊅ J3)*

Jamie Oliver has opened a branch of his British mini-chain in Amsterdam. The cocktail bar at the entrance starts things off well. In the trattoria you can eat well à la carte without breaking the bank, and the restaurant dishes up a four-course menu for 46 euros. Don't expect to see Jamie himself, but at least the recipes are his. *Daily | Jollemanhof 9 | tel. 0900 3 43 83 36 | tram 26 Kattenburgerstraat*

INSIDER TIP ▶ GARTINE ☺ (120 B5) *(⊅ F4)*

Breakfast and lunch restaurant, hidden in a side street off Kalverstraat. The owners serve produce from their own vegetable garden and the region, from beef salad with roast pumpkin to sausage made from Beemsterland pork. *Closed Mon–Tue | Taksteeg 7 | tel. 020 3 20 41 32 | tram 4, 9, 14, 16, 24, 25 Spui*

GOLDEN TEMPLE ☺ (128 B2) *(⊅ G5)*

This vegetarian eatery mixes its styles: Indian, Arab and Mexican dishes can all be had. No smoking, no meat, no alcohol – nothing at all to harm your health. It is run by Sikhs, who are pleased to cater for vegans. *Daily | Utrechtsestraat 126 | tel. 020 6 26 85 60 | tram 4, 7, 10 Frederiksplein*

DE GOUDEN REAEL (123 E2) *(⊅ F1)*

Rustic French cooking in a 17th-century building. The oven-roasted leg of lamb is a treat. *Daily | Zandhoek 14 | tel. 020 6 23 38 83 | bus 28 Barentszplein*

Vegetarian treat at Fifteen

HARKEMA (120 B4) *(⊅ G4)*

The brick exterior of a former tobacco factory conceals a huge restaurant with modern design that pulls in a trendy crowd. The food is international, but that's not what it's all about: you come here to feast on the interior design. *Daily |Nes 67 | tel. 020 4 28 22 22 | tram 4, 9, 16, 24, 25 Dam*

HOI TIN ★ (121 D3) *(⊅ G3)*

A big restaurant in Chinatown. At lunchtime you sit among Chinese families who are enjoying a proper feast. The menu doesn't pander to European tastes, but has a range of authentic specialities. Good selection of dim sum. *Daily | Zeedijk 122–124 | tel. 020 6 25 64 51 | Metro Nieuwmarkt*

JAPANESE PANCAKE WORLD (123 D4) *(⊅ E3)*

And you thought pancakes were a Dutch speciality! Think again – they are a popular form of fast food in Japan. Here guests can watch as calorie-rich Asian pancakes are conjured up in front of their eyes. *closed Mon | 2e Egelantiersdwarsstraat 24a | tel. 020 3 20 44 47 | www. japanesepancakeworld.com | tram 13, 14, 17 Westermarkt*

LE ZINC ... ET LES AUTRES (128 B1) (*ቢ G5*)
Behind the façade of a 17th-century warehouse on Prinsengracht some sophisticated French cuisine is produced, but the crowning glory of an evening here is the cheeseboard, and then it's time to try some Dutch specialities. *Closed Sun | Prinsengracht 999 | tel. 020 6 22 90 44 | tram 4 Prinsengracht*

LIEVE (120 A2) (*ቢ F3*)
If there is one thing the Dutch appreciate about the Belgians, it's their cooking. Come to Lieve to find out why. The tasting menu of Belgian beer goes well with venison paté or monkfish. *Daily | Herengracht 88 | tel. 020 6 24 96 35 | tram 13, 14, 17 Raadhuisstraat*

MEMORIES OF INDIA (120 B6) (*ቢ G5*)
This is an offshoot of the London restaurant of the same name. Papadoms with chutney make the time spent waiting for a table palatable. Bear in mind here that when they describe a dish as hot here, they really mean it. *Daily | Reguliersdwarsstraat 88 | tel. 020 6 23 57 10 | tram 4, 9, 14 Rembrandtplein*

MOEDERS ★ (123 D5) (*ቢ E4*)
Home food just the way mum cooks – and to make the point the walls are covered with hundreds of photos of mothers. The menu is traditionally Dutch, but there are a few dishes that might have been rustled up by a Mediterranean mamma. *Daily | Rozengracht 251 | tel.*

020 6 26 79 57 | tram 10, 13, 14, 17 Marnixstraat or Rozengracht

MORITA-YA ★ (121 D2) (*ቢ G3*)
Eating Japanese doesn't have to be expensive, as this little place shows. What they save on the decor goes into the quality of the fish and sushi. *Closed Mon | Zeedijk 18 | tel. 020 6 38 07 56 | Metro Nieuwmarkt*

NEW KING (121 D3) (*ቢ G3*)
A Chinese with dim interior design, which is always bursting at the seems. Chinese classics, but also meals that are rarely found from eggplant with tofu to filled cuttlefish. *Daily. | Zeedijk 115–117 | tel. 020 6 25 21 80 | Metro Nieuwmarkt*

PATA NEGRA ★ (128 B1) (*ቢ G5*)
Spain in Amsterdam: walk through the door of this noisy, bustling, always crowded tapas restaurant, and you'll think you've been beamed to Seville. Beneath the hams hanging from the ceiling are simple wooden benches, and the wine is served in ceramic jugs. *Daily | Utrechtsestraat 124 | tel. 020 4 22 62 50 | tram 4 Prinsengracht*

INSIDER TIP ▶ PROEF (122 C2) (*ቢ D1*)
The transformer hall of the Westergasfabriek (gasworks) is where Marije Vogelzang creates her 'designs for eating'. Everything is charmingly unconventional and a real experience: juice is served in jam jars, and you snip at the herbs yourself with scissors. No credit cards, only debit. *Closed Mon | Gosschalklaan 12 | tel. 020 6 82 26 56 | tram 110 Van Hallstraat*

INSIDER TIP ▶ REM EILAND (0) (*ቢ 0*)
A curiosity in the old wood harbour (Oude Houthaven): in the 1960s this tower construction stood in the North Sea and housed

a pirate transmitter, later it served as a water measurement station. In 2011 it was relocated to the wood harbour and converted into a restaurant with a panoramic view. Meals of modern Dutch and Mediterranean kitchen. *Daily | Haparandad-*

the meat is organic. *Daily | Keizersgracht 312 | tel. 020 4 23 38 17 | tram 13, 14, 17 Westermarkt*

TUJUH MARET ★ (128 B1) (*ω G5*)
Authentic Indonesian cooking based

Authentic tapas restaurant in the heart of Amsterdam: Pata Negra

am 45 | tel. 020 6 88 55 01 | bus 22, 48 Oostzaanstraat

SAMBA KITCHEN (128 A3) (*ω F7*)
See if you can still do the samba after this Brazilian treat: for a fixed price of 27.50 euros you eat as much grilled and marinated meat, plus side dishes, as you want. *Daily | Ceintuurbaan 63 | tel. 020 6 76 05 13 | tram 3, 12, 25 Ferdinand Bolstraat*

DE STRUISVOGEL ☺ (123 D5) (*ω F4*)
Cosy cellar with good bistro food. Various three-course menus for 23 euros, and all

on the food of the Minahasa region in the north of Sulawesi. If you'd like to sample a bit of everything, order one of the *rijsttafels* for two. *Daily | Utrechtsestraat 73 | tel. 020 4 27 98 65 | tram 4 Keizersgracht*

YAM YAM (122 C4) (*ω D3*)
The best if not the cheapest pizza in Amsterdam: a proper thin base, topped with rocket, Parma ham or ceps. Make sure you still have room for a wonderful dessert: the home-made ice cream with pistachios and honey. *Closed Mon | Frederik*

With all the colour of the bazaar around you, it has to be oriental food

Hendrikstraat 90 | tel. 020 6 81 50 97 | tram 3 Frederik Hendrikplein

RESTAURANTS: BUDGET

DE AARDIGE PERS (122 C4) (📍 E3)

This Persian restaurant lives up to its name, 'the friendly Persian', and at weekends is often packed with extended Persian families. You should definitely try the chicken with walnuts and pomegranate syrup. *Daily | 2e Hugo de Grootstraat 13 | tel. 020 4 00 31 07 | tram 3 Hugo de Grootplein*

BAZAR (128 B3) (📍 G6)

Oriental restaurant on Albert Cuypmarkt, furnished with lots of Arabian kitsch. A big, noisy place with a cheerful atmosphere where you can get an oriental breakfast from 9am. *Daily | Albert Cuyp-straat 182 | tel. 020 6 75 05 44 | tram 16, 24 Albert Cuypstraat*

BEYROUTH (122 C6) (📍 E4)

Hummus, falafel, lamb pasties and much more: if you order the mezze starter at this likeable Lebanese restaurant, before you know it there will be 15 different dishes on the table. *Closed Mon | Kinkerstraat 18 | tel. 020 6 16 06 35 | tram 7, 10, 17 Elandsgracht*

BIRD (121 D2) (📍 G3)

The walls are decorated with pictures of the king and queen of Thailand, and the sound system puts forth Asian pop music. This takeaway is colourful, jolly and anything but quiet. Which means you won't confuse it with the much more expensive restaurant of the same name that's opposite! *Daily | Zeedijk 77 | tel. 020 4 20 62 89 | Metro Nieuwmarkt*

DE BRAKKE GROND (120 B4) (*ULI G4*)
Popular place to dine in the Flemish cultural centre. Downstairs it's a buzzing pub, upstairs a quieter restaurant. *Daily | Nes 43 | tel. 020 6 26 00 44 | tram all except 3, 7, 12, 26 Dam*

CHANG EXPRESS (121 D2) (*ULI G3*)
Surinamese run this snack bar. They dish up Surinamese food such as *moksi meti* (smoked meat with rice) or chicken pancakes. *Daily | Nieuwebrugsteeg 16 | 5 min. on foot from the main station | tel. 020 4 20 78 84*

KADIJK (121 F4) (*ULI H4*)
From outside it looks like a normal café, but the menu lists affordable Indonesian specialities. The mackerel is delicious. *Daily | Kadijksplein 5 | tel. 020 1 77 44 41 | 10 min. on foot from the main station*

NAM KEE (121 D3) (*ULI G3*)
The Dutch hit film The Oysters of Nam Kee made this Chinese restaurant a legend. Simple food at a reasonable price, tasty noodle soup and service that's more efficient than friendly. *Daily | Zeedijk 111 | tel. 020 6 24 34 07 | Metro Nieuwmarkt*

PALOMA BLANCA (126 C1) (*ULI D5*)
Sweet peppermint tea and delicious couscous, if no alcohol, are on offer at this Moroccan restaurant. *Closed Mon | Jan Pieter Heijestraat 145 | tel. 020 7 71 46 06 | tram 7, 10 Jan Pieter Heijestraat*

INSIDER TIP PANCAKES! (123 D5) (*ULI F4*)
A very small pancake restaurant in a shopping street. Delicious thin pancakes in a child-friendly environment. No reservations! *Daily | Berenstraat 38 | tram 13, 14, 17 Westermarkt*

THE SEAFOOD BAR ☺ (127 E2) (*ULI E5*)
Fish restaurant near Museumplein, in which you can order a three course meal as well as fish & chips and small tidbits – not only fresh off the boat but also from sustainable breeding and fisheries. No reservations! *Daily | Van Baerlestraat 5 | tram 2, 3, 5, 12 Van Baerlestraat*

SEMHAR (122 C4) (*ULI E3*)
Spicy Ethiopian dishes that you scoop up with a piece of pancake with your hands instead of a knife and fork. Wash it down with banana beer and INSIDER TIP mocha with incense. *Daily | Marnixstraat 259–261 | tel. 020 6 38 16 34 | tram 3, 10 Westerstraat*

LOW BUDGET

▶ A street stall called *Vlaamse Friethuis (Daily. | (120 B5) (*ULI E4*) (Voetboogstraat 31 | tram 1, 2, 5 Koningsplein)* sells the best French fries in all Amsterdam, which is why there is often a long queue. Choose between 20 (!) kinds of mayonnaise.

▶ Surinamese breadrolls are exotic, delicious and affordable. *Tjin's (128 C2) (*ULI G6*) (daily | Van Woustraat 17 | tram 4, 25 Stadhouderskade)* offers food starting at 4 euros, for example a sandwich topped with pickled beef and stringbeans.

▶ Arabian chickpea balls in pita bread, and as much as you want to take from the salad buffet, that's the deal at *Maoz Falafel (120 B5) (*ULI G4*) (daily | Muntplein 1 | tram 4, 9, 16, 24, 25 Muntplein)*

SHOPPING

CITY **WHERE TO START?**
    Amsterdam's most charac-
terful shopping area is **9 Straatjes (123 D–E5)** *(⌀ E–F4)*, nine
little streets that run from west
to east between Westermarkt
and Leidsegracht: Reestraat,
Runstraat, Berenstraat and their
continuations. It's an area of little
shops with a big selectioin, from
designer fashion to art books,
from junk to Dutch cheese – and
lots of nice cafés. The nearest
tram stops for the 9 straatjes are
Westermarkt (tram 13, 14, 17),
Dam (tram 1, 2, 5, 13, 14, 17) and
Spui (tram 1, 2, 5).

**Amsterdam is wonderland for shoppers.
The city centre shops open on Sundays,
and the sales assistants are astonish-
ingly friendly even when it gets really
hectic.**

The epicentre of the shopping action is
the triangle formed by Dam, Muntplein
and Leidseplein. In the Kalvertoren and
● Magna Plaza shopping centres, you
can hunt bargains in comfort even
when it rains. But what really makes
Amsterdam attractive to shoppers are
all the little stores, which are known as
winkels. There is a diverse mix of this
kind of shops and pleasant cafés in the
9 straatjes as well as in Utrechtsestraat
and on the Haarlemmerdijk. Around
Museumplein, especially in P. C. Hooft-
straat, you will find the high-class ad-

Photo: In the designercollective shop Droog Design

Winkelen in shopping heaven:
Plenty of little shops make Amsterdam
a truly enjoyable retail experience

dresses: international designer labels and luxury boutiques have moved in here. If design for modern living is your weakness, Rozengracht is the place to go.

It is also worth visiting the markets, especially Albert Cuypmarkt, where you are sure to find something nice to take home. The international flavour of Amsterdam is apparent in the ● *tokos,* exotic little shops selling Thai, Surinamese and Indian food, which can also be found close to Albert Cuypmarkt.

ANTIQUES

EDUARD KRAMER ★ (128 A1) (*🛍 F5*)
Antique Dutch tiles in every price range, from Baroque to Art Nouveau, from blue-and-white to colourful. *Nieuwe Spiegelstraat 64 | www.antique-tileshop. nl | tram 16, 24, 25 Vijzelgracht*

DE LOOIER (123 D5) (*🛍 E4*)
De Looier is the largest covered antiques market in the Netherlands. Its building on Lijnbaansgracht houses over 70

FLOWERS

stands and several shops, though some of the stands are hardly bigger than a showcase. They sell everything from porcelain to toys and furniture. *Elandsgracht 109 | tram 7, 10, 17 Elandsgracht*

FLOWERS

JEMI (120 C2) (*📖 G3*)

If you thought the only thing to do with cut flowers is stick them in a vase, you'll learn something here. You can eat them too, or make bags and clothes out of them. *Warmoesstraat 83 a | tram 4, 9, 16, 24, 25 Beurs van Berlage*

BOOKS

ATHENAEUM (120 A5) (*📖 F4*)

One of the city's best-stocked bookstores, and the adjoining newsagent's has a huge range of magazines. *Spui 14–16 | tram 1, 2, 5 Spui*

BOEKENMARKT OUDEMANHUISPOORT ⭐ (120 C4–5) (*📖 G4*)

This book market is located well sheltered in an 18th century arcade in the university quarter. *Oudemanhuispoort | tram 4, 9, 14, 16, 24, 25 Rokin*

LAMBIEK (127 F1) (*📖 F5*)

Europe's oldest shop for second-hand comics. As well as the comics themselves, posters and original drawings, mainly by Dutch artists, are on sale. *Kerkstraat 132 | www.lambiek.net | tram 16, 24, 25 Keizersgracht*

EATABLES

DE BIERKONING (120 B3) (*📖 F3*)

300 different beer glasses and 900 brews from all over the world to pour into them, including obscure regional beers, justify the 'beer king's' name. *Paleisstraat 125 | www.bierkoning.nl | tram 1, 2, 5, 13, 14, 17 Dam*

JACOB HOOY & CO ⭐ (120 C4) (*📖 G3*)

Entering this spice shop is like taking a trip back in time. 500 kinds of herbs and spices, stored in wooden drawers and barrels labelled in gold lettering, fill the space with their aromas. Behind the counter you see 30 jars of *drop* – salty or sweet Dutch liquorice. *Kloveniersburgwal 10–12 | Metro Nieuwmarkt*

INSIDER TIP ▶ KAASHUIS TROMP (128 B1) (*📖 G5*)

Dutch and international cheese is piled to the rafters in this little shop on Utrechtsestraat. The staff is ready to help and will let you try them before you

Creativity with plants by Jemi

buy. *Utrechtsestraat 90 | tram 4 Prinsengracht*

MARQT ★ ⌚ (123 F6) (*Ⓜ G4*)

A fashionable supermarket that sells only eco-friendly and regional products. Buy something to take home such as cheese, salty liquorice or beer from local breweries, or pick up a fresh pizza and salad to eat straight away. *Utrechtsestraat 17 | tram 4, 9, 14 Rembrandtplein*

INSIDER TIP PUCCINI
(120 C5) (*Ⓜ G4*)

Puccini's chocolates are big, unusual and unbelievably enticing. In this stylishly furnished shop they think nothing of giving chocolate a scent of thyme, lemongrass or gin. *Staalstraat 17 | tram 9, 14 Waterlooplein*

GALLERIES

GALERIE FONS WELTERS ●
(123 D4) (*Ⓜ E3*)

This gallery is dedicated to contemporary Dutch art, much of it too big to carry. *Bloemstraat 140 | tram 13, 14, 17 Westermarkt*

REFLEX GALERIE (127 F2) (*Ⓜ F5*)

This gallery opposite the Rijksmuseum specialises in contemporary photography with a difference. *Weteringschans 79a | tram 6, 7, 10 Spiegelstraat*

DEPARTMENT STORES

BIJENKORF ★ (120 B3) (*Ⓜ F3*)

The best-known chain of department stores (the name means 'beehive') in the Netherlands was founded in 1870, and this one on the Dam was built in 1915. Everything here is that little bit classier. *Dam 1 | tram all routes (Dam) except 3, 7, 10, 12*

INSIDER TIP HEMA
(120 B5) (*Ⓜ F4*)

What used to be a very basic store has become a kind of Dutch Ikea. Reasonably priced goods with minimalist, often amazingly good design. *e.g. in the Kalvertoren shopping centre (Kalverstraat | Heiligeweg | Tram 4, 9, 14, 16, 24, 25 Muntplein)*

★ **Eduard Kramer**
Old Dutch tiles in every colour for every budget → p. 69

★ **Boekenmarkt Oudemanhuispoort**
Old books in a historic arcade → p. 70

★ **Jacob Hooy & Co**
Filled with the aromas of spice and tea → p. 70

★ **Marqt**
Supermarket devoted to regional and organic products → p. 71

★ **Bijenkorf**
Traditional department store on the Dam → p. 71

★ **Albert Cuypmarkt**
Multicultural outdoor market → p. 72

★ **Heinen Delft ware**
Genuine Royal Delft and other hand-painted porcelain → p. 74

★ **Hajenius**
This cigar smokers' paradise has wood panelling and crystal chandeliers → p. 75

MARCO POLO HIGHLIGHTS

THIS & THAT

MAISON DE BONNETERIE
(120 B5) (*∅ F4*)

Long-established, top-of-the-range store. Haute couture for ladies and gentlemen. The old building has a beautiful **INSIDER TIP** inner courtyard. *Rokin 140–142 | tram 4, 9, 14, 16, 24, 25 Muntplein*

THIS & THAT

KITSCH KITCHEN SUPERMERCADO
(123 D4) (*∅ E3*)

Everything here has garish colours and crazy patterns: amusing household items from developing-world countries. *Rozengracht 8–12 | tram 13, 14, 17 Westermarkt*

PERFUMES OF THE PAST
(123 E3) (*∅ F2*)

A tiny shop, but it stocks just about every classic perfume. *Binnen Oranistraat 11 | 10 min. on foot from the main station*

DE WITTE TANDEN WINKEL
(123 D5) (*∅ F4*)

You'll find nothing but toothbrushes in this *winkel*, from unusual models for toothbrush freaks to special devices for dental hygiene. *Runstraat 5 | tram 13, 14, 17 Westermarkt*

MARKETS

ALBERT CUYPMARKT ★
(128 B3) (*∅ F–G6*)

Amsterdam's biggest and best-known outdoor market is truly multicultural. See, smell and buy vegetables, fish, cheese, spices and flowers, as well as Indian fabrics and African hair gel. *Mon–Sat 9.30am–5pm | tram 16, 24 Albert Cuypstraat; 4, 25 Stadhouderskade*

Caps, sunglasses, fabrics, fish – it's all to be had at Albert Cuypmarkt

FLOWER MARKET (120 A–B5) (*ɰ F4*)
Here they sell everything to send gardeners into a state of bliss: flower bulbs, houseplants and balcony flowers – though the prices might make you take a deep breath. *Mon–Sat 9.30am–5pm | Singel | tram 1, 2, 4, 5 Koningsplein; 9, 14, 16, 24, 25 Muntplein*

NOORDERMARKT (123 E3) (*ɰ F2*)
Around the Noorderkerk there are flea market stands on Mondays and organic food on Saturdays. You can combine a stroll along the ☺ organic market with a visit to the food stalls on adjoining Lindengracht. *Mon 9am–4pm flea market, Sat 9am–4pm organic produce | Noordermarkt and Westerstraat | tram 13, 14, 17 Westermarkt*

WATERLOOPLEIN (121 D5) (*ɰ G4*)
The city's only regular flea market is on Waterlooplein. It sells everything imaginable, from bike tyres and inner tubes to incense burners and second-hand leather jackets. *Mon–Sat 10am–5pm | Waterlooplein | tram 9, 14 | Metro Waterlooplein*

FASHION & ACCESSORIES

MARLIES DEKKERS (123 D5) (*ɰ F4*)
Flagship store of the grande dame of fashionable Dutch underwear. Extremely sexy lingerie without frills is presented in luxurious Snow White-style surroundings. *Berenstraat 18 | tram 13, 14, 17 Westermarkt*

INDIVIDUALS (120 B5) (*ɰ F4*)
Twice a year 13 Amsterdam students of fashion design present a new collection here. Stylists and fashion editors come here in search of new talent. *Spui 23 | tram 1, 2, 4, 5, 9, 14, 16, 24, 25 Spui*

JAN (123 F6) (*ɰ G5*)
Designer bits and bobs, from handbags and jewellery to lifestyle books and accessories for the home. *Utrechtsestraat 74 | tram 4 Keizersgracht*

INSIDER TIP ▶ **JUTKA & RISKA (122 C5)** (*ɰ D4*)
A little bit out of the way, but if vintage fashion and accessories from the 1970s and 1980s make your pulse race, combined with new items designed by sisters Jutka and Riska Volkerts' own label, it's worth the trip. *Bilderdijkstraat 194 | tram 3, 7, 10, 12, 14, 17 Bilderdijkstraat*

FRANS MOLENAAR (127 E2) (*ɰ E6*)
Legendary Dutch avant-garde designer whose clothes have stayed true to his preference for clear lines and geometric patterns since the 1960s. *Jan Luyckenstraat 104 | tram 2, 5 Hobbemakade*

NUKUHIVA ☺ (123 E3) (*ɰ G2*)
You might not notice when you look at the jeans and basics here, but this little boutique specialises in fair-trade fashion. Part of the profits goes to educational projects in the developing world. *Haarlemmerstraat 36 | 10 min. on foot from the main station*

SISSY BOY (125 E4) (*ɰ L3*)
A Dutch fashion chain that also sells accessories for the home. Come here for dresses or for beautiful scarves made by *Jago. KNSM-laan 19 | tram 10 Azartplein*

SPRMRKT (123 D5) (*ɰ E4*)
New designer fashion, used designer furniture and all kinds of trendy accessories in a barn-like store on Rozengracht. *Rozengracht 191–193 | tram 13, 14, 17 Marnixstraat*

JEWELLERY & DIAMONDS

JEWELLERY & DIAMONDS

INSIDER TIP YDU – YOUNG DESIGNERS UNITED (123 E6) *(𝔐 F4)*
Unknown young designers can rent space on the racks here to sell their creative work. They guarantee that there are no more than four of each piece. *Keizersgracht 447 | tram 1, 2, 5 Keizersgracht*

JEWELLERY & DIAMONDS

Most jewellers can be found on Lange-brugsteeg and Grimburgwal (near Munt-plein).

GASSAN DAM SQUARE
(120 B3) *(𝔐 F3)*
If you're passing by, pop in and buy some: this big diamond dealer is located right on the Dam. Apart from sparkling gemstones you can pick up a high-end

wristwatch. *Rokin 1–5 | tram all routes Dam except 3, 7, 10, 12*

LIJFERING & ROS (120 C4) *(𝔐 G4)*
Paul Lijfering and Angelique Ros lovingly restore Art Nouveau jewellery and old watches. *Oudemanhuispoort 1a | tram 9, 14, 16, 24, 25 Muntplein*

SHOES

JAN JANSEN (120 B4) *(𝔐 F4)*
Internationally known shoe designer whose extravagant works have even been exhibited in the Stedelijk Museum. *Rokin 42 | tram 4, 9, 14, 16, 24, 25 Rokin*

INSIDER TIP OTTEN & ZOON
(128 B3) *(𝔐 F6)*
Established since 1898 in a side street off Albert Cuypmarkt: a shop for genuine clogs and other healthy shoes, and definitely not at tourist prices. *1e van der Helststraat 31 | tram 16, 24, 25 Albert Cuypmarkt*

INSIDER TIP UNITED NUDE
(120 A4) *(𝔐 F4)*
Dutch shoe design with a flair for eye-catching heels by the nephew of famous architect Rem Koolhaas. *Spuistraat 125A | tram 1, 2, 5 Spui*

ZWARTJES VAN 1883 (128 B1) *(𝔐 G5)*
Long-established shoe shop with a touch of class. It attracts customers who want quality and comfort. *Utrechtsestraat 123 | tram 4 Keizersgracht*

SOUVENIRS

HEINEN DELFTWARE ★
(127 F1) *(𝔐 F3)*
Father Jaap and son Joris paint some of the porcelain themselves, but also sell products from the Royal Delft porcelain

LOW BUDGET

▶ For lower prices if less picturesque surroundings than on Albert Cuypmarkt go to *Dappermarkt* **(129 E1)** *(𝔐 K5)* *(Mon–Sat 10am–4.30pm | Dapperstraat | tram 14 Pontanusstraat | tram 9 1e from Swindenstraat)* in Dapperstraat.

▶ In Dutch supermarkets *exotic spices* are much cheaper than elsewhere in Europe. As Indonesia was once a Dutch colony, the choice is enormous – from dried lemongrass to cumin and fenugreek.

▶ Buy flowers and flower bulbs on the street markets that sell food! They cost half as much as on the flower market on Singel!

manufactory. *Prinsengracht 440 | tram 13, 14, 17 Westermarkt*

THINKING OF HOLLAND
(124 B4) (*IIJ J3*)

Would you believe it? A souvenir shop with no clogs or tulip bulbs. Instead they have a big range of original items for wearing and living by Dutch designers, ranging in price from cheap to exclusive. *Piet Heinkade 23 (in the cruise ship terminal) | tram 25, 26 Muziekgebouw*

TOBACCO

HAJENIUS ★ (120 B4) (*IIJ F4*)

Tobacco, cigarettes and hand-rolled cigars have been sold since 1826 in the elegant Empire interior of this long-established tobacconist's shop with its wood panelling and crystal chandeliers. *Rokin 92 | tram 4, 9, 14, 16, 24, 25 Rokin*

DESIGN FOR THE HOME

DROOG@HOME (120 C5) (*IIJ G4*)

In the mid-1990s Droog Design made a name for itself with an experimental look. A few years ago the designers' collective set up its own shop and gallery. *Staalstraat 7b | tram 9, 14 Waterlooplein*

INSIDER TIP FROZEN FOUNTAIN
(123 D6) (*IIJ F4*)

Unconventional forms for everything from chairs to lamps. Nothing is off the peg, and that has its price. *Prinsengracht 645 | tram 1, 2, 5, 7, 10 Raamplein*

WAAR 😊 (120 B5) (*IIJ F4*)

Fair-trade shop with an emphasis on design. At Waar you can buy not only fair-trade food but also crockery, vases, basket and bathroom accessories with a modern and minimalist style. *Heiligeweg 45 | tram 1, 2, 5 (Koningsplein)*

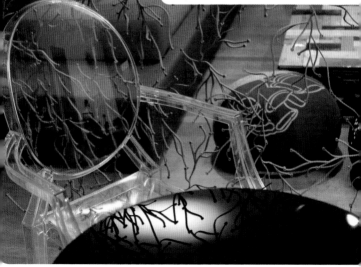

Design encounters of the third kind: Frozen Fountain

ENTERTAINMENT

CITY WHERE TO START?
Amsterdams somewhat chaotic square **Leidseplein (123 D6)** *(⌖ E5)* is the focus of entertainment in Amsterdam. All around it there is pulsating city life in the evening: in lots of pubs, as well as cinemas, theatres and clubs. The Stadsschouwburg, Kino City and the De Balie arts centre stand directly on the square. Clubs like Jimmy Woo and Sugar Factory are hidden away in the narrow streets around Leidseplein, and it's not far to Paradiso and Melkweg. The best way to get there is by tram routes 1, 2, 3, 5, 7, 10 and 13 stop at Leidseplein.

Amsterdam never seems to sleep, especially at weekends. The city centre is abuzz all night long: taxis and cyclists jam the narrow streets, and in summer the countless outdoor cafés are packed. The hotspots for nightlife are Leidseplein and Rembrandtplein. Around Spui and Nieuwmarkt and in the De Pijp quarter the action is less touristy.

The traditional way to kick off the evening is *borreluur:* an after-office rendezvous when colleagues repair to a ‚brown café', i.e. a wood-panelled pub, for beer and snacks. For cultural entertainment there is a host of theatres, though most performances are in Dutch. For an evening out without language barrier, visitors can attend performances by famous Dutch dance

---

Photo: Nieuwmarkt in the evening

Borreluur, music and canal trips: there's almost more going on in the city centre after dark than during the day

and music ensembles such as the *Concertgebouw Orchestra* or *Nederlands Dans Theater*. Make your booking in good time, as tickets are seldom available at the last minute. For information, advance sales and reservations go to the *Amsterdam Tourist Office (p. 109)*. There is a huge range of pop concerts, and no shortage of clubbing venues. Cocktail bars, on the other hand, are few and far between, as Amsterdamers generally prefer to drink beer in a cosy pub.

BARS

NOL (123 D3) (*ℳ F3*)

Genuine Jordaan bar with flowered wallpaper and crystal chandeliers. The regulars often sing along to Dutch hits played over the sound system. *Westerstraat 109 | tram 3 Marnixplein*

INSIDER TIP SKYLOUNGE ☼
(124 A4) (*ℳ H3*)

The Skylounge on the 11th floor of the Doubletree hotel is worth a visit not

Try them all: over 200 kinds of beer at In de Wildeman

so much for it its atmosphere as for its breathtaking view of the old city, the harbour and IJ – day and night. *Daily 11amm–1am Uhr | Oosterdoksstraat 4 | 5 Min. walk from the main trainstation*

SUPPERCLUB BAR (120 B3) *(🕮 F4)*
A blood-red bar and a dazzling white lounge where the beautiful people come to hear what DJs play at the weekend and recorded soft music the rest of the week. *Jonge Roelensteeg 21 | tram all routes Dam except 3, 7, 10, 12*

TWENTY THIRD BAR
(128 B4) *(🕮 F7)*
Following a refurbishment, what used to be an old-fashioned cocktail bar on the 23rd floor of the Okura Hotel has become a trendy lounge bar. And the unbeatable panorama is of course as amazing as it always was. The Michelin-starred *Ciel Bleu* restaurant next door provides exclusive snacks. *Ferdinand Bolstraat 333 | tram 24, 25 Cornelis Troostplein*

CAFÉS & PUBS

During the week most cafés and pubs open until 1am, at weekends two hours longer.

DE BALIE (127 F1) *(🕮 F5)*
Big café, small restaurant and arts centre on Leidseplein. The café fills up before and after lectures or film screenings in the adjacent halls. *Kleine Gartmanplantsoen | tram 1, 2, 5, 6, 7, 10 Leidseplein*

BROUWERIJ 'T IJ (125 F6) *(🕮 K4)*
One of Amsterdam's few beer gardens is located right by a historic windmill. The mill is home to the local t'IJ brewery, which makes 100 % organic and unfiltered beer. *Daily | Funenkade 7 | tram 10 (Hoogte Kadijk), 14 (Pontanusstraat)*

DE OOSTERLING ● (128 B2) *(🕮 G5)*
Traditional pub with genuine Amsterdam regulars, family-run for 100 years. Rustic wooden fittings, a good range of beers, no music. *Utrechtsestraat 140 | tram 4, 6, 7, 10 Frederiksplein*

VYNE (123 D5) *(🕮 F4)*
Wine is what it's all about here. Refrigerators full of bottles line the entire left-hand side of the room. *Prinsengracht 411 | tram 13, 14, 17 Westermarkt*

IN DE WILDEMAN ★ (120 C2) *(🕮 G3)*
Watering hole in an old distillery that looks like a cross between a pub and an old-fashioned pharmacy. Over 200 kinds

of beer, 17 of them on draught. *Closed Sun | Kolksteeg 3 | tram 1, 2, 5 Kolk*

INSIDER TIP WYNAND FOCKINK
(120 B3) (*Ш G4*)

A tiny *proeflokaal* (tasting parlour) dating from 1679 in a covered alleyway near the Krasnapolsky Hotel. Behind it is the distillery in which 60 kinds of schnapps are made. Closes at 9pm! *Pijlsteeg 31 | tram all routes except 3, 7, 12, 26 Dam*

CLUBS & DISCOS

Amsterdam has a fairly laid-back clubbing scene: dress codes hardly exist, and the guys on the door are on the whole not really a problem. Sometimes you have to wait patiently to get in though.

CLUB AIR (120 G6) (*Ш C4*)

A big club with electronic beats of the experimental kind. A prepaid system simplifies paying at the bar. *Amstelstra-* at 16 | *www.air.nl | tram 4, 9, 14 Rembrandtplein*

INSIDER TIP CLUB TROUW
(129 D3) (*Ш H6*)

On the upper floor of a former newspaper printworks you can start the evening with a meal and dance later on in a bare, industrial atmosphere, usually to electronic sounds. *Wibautstraat 127 | www. trouwamsterdam.nl | Metro Wibautstraat*

ESCAPE (120 C6) (*Ш G4*)

One of the city's biggest clubs, accommodating up to 2500 guests. Be prepared to wait for admission at weekends, and when you get to the door there's no guarantee they'll let you in. *Rembrandtplein 11am–3pm | admission from 12 euros | www.escape.nl | tram 4 Rembrandtplein*

JIMMY WOO ★ (127 F1) (*Ш E5*)

Cool location with a Chinese touch. Beneath more than 12,000 lamps Amsterdam's young and beautiful crowd groove to house music on an

---

★ **In de Wildeman**
A choice made difficult: in this ancient *proeflokaal* (tasting room) you can try 200 kinds of beer
→ p. 78

★ **Jimmy Woo**
Chinese star in the Amsterdam night sky → p. 79

★ **Paradiso**
Pop, rock and techno where hymns were once sung → p. 80

★ **Canal trips**
A true Amsterdam experience: glide along canals after dark → p. 80

★ **Tuschinski**
A fabulous old cinema – inside and outside → p. 81

★ **Concertgebouw**
One of the world's top orchestras benefits from superb acoustics
→ p. 82

★ **Het Muziektheater**
Something for every mood: from experimental dance to grand opera
→ p. 83

★ **Stadsschouwburg**
Palace of drama on Leidseplein with an extensive programme → p. 83

MARCO POLO HIGHLIGHTS

enormous dance floor. In the lounge you can chill out on black leather sofas between Asian antiques. *Korte Leidsedwarsstraat 18 | admission from 10 euros | www.jimmywoo.com | tram 1, 2, 5, 6, 7, 10 Leidseplein*

MELKWEG (127 F1) (*Ø E5*)

A legendary arts centre in a converted dairy. Changing programme of concerts, disco, films and exhibitions. *Café from 1pm, meals served 6–9pm | Lijnbaansgracht 234 | admission 4–15 euros depending on the event | www.melkweg.nl | tram 1, 2, 5, 6, 7, 10 Leidseplein*

PARADISO ⭐ (127 F1) (*Ø F5*)

This location has been renowned for decades: a dance club and stage for concerts in a converted church, a fixture in the nightlife of Amsterdam since the days when punk was the latest trend. Changing programme of events, techno DJs at weekends. *Weteringschans 6–8 | admission up to 20 euros | www.paradiso.nl | tram 1, 2, 5, 6, 7, 10 Leidseplein*

SUGAR FACTORY (127 F1) (*Ø E5*)

A small all-round club near Leidseplein, a venue for DJ sets but also theatre productions and art performances. The musical offerings range from electro to jazz and world music. *Lijnbaansgracht 238 | admission: from 8.50 euros | www.sugarfactory.nl | tram 1, 2, 5, 7, 10 Leidseplein*

WESTERUNIE (122 C2) (*Ø D1*)

JEvery weekend Dutch DJs do their stuff in a hall of the old Westergasfabrik (gasworks). The huge, 12-metre-high hall holds up to 800 revellers. *Klönneplein 4 | www.westerunie.nl | tram 10 Van Hallstraat*

CANAL TRIPS

⭐ Glide along the canals at night – what could be more romantic? The boat operated by *Rederij Lovers (Tue–Sat 7, 8 and 9pm | Prins Hendrikkade 25–27, opposite the main station | tel. 020 5 30 10 90 | 14 euros)* spends an hour passing illuminated bridges and the façades of canal-side houses in the historic quarter. Here and there you get a glimpse of the scene inside a lit-up houseboat.

As an alternative you can book a *Redlight Candlelight Cruise (Tue–Sat 8pm| 32.50 euros)* including wine, snacks, a genever tasting and a short walk through the red-light district.

JAZZ CLUBS

BIMHUIS (124 B3) (*Ø H3*)

Internationally renowned jazz venue, founded in 1974 and now housed in a spectacular new waterfront building. Mon–Wed jam sessions from 10pm. *Closed July and Aug | Piet Heinkade 3 | 5 min. on foot from the main station | tel. 020 788 2188*

CASABLANCA (121 D2) *(𝄞 G3)*

The oldest and probably the most famous jazz club in the Netherlands. Back in 1945 the war generation danced to the sounds of Kit Dynamite and other jazz greats of the era. Sat and Sun 'Open Podium'. *Zeedijk 26 | 5 min. on foot from the main station*

JAZZ CAFÉ ALTO (127 F1) *(𝄞 F5)*

Look out for the big saxophone sign on the front of the building. The intimate *Café Alto* near Leidseplein stages live jazz seven evenings per week. Tuesday is Latino night, and every Wednesday saxophone legend Hans Dulfer performs. *Korte Leidsedwarsstraat 115 | www.jazz-cafe-alto.nl | tram 1, 2, 5, 6, 7, 10 Leidseplein*

CASINO

HOLLAND CASINO (127 F1) *(𝄞 E5)*

A striking round building is home to one of the world's most modern casinos. If you are over 18 and properly dressed, you can play roulette, blackjack, poker, etc. beneath a colourful glass dome. A restaurant and dance floor are also on site. *Max Euweplein 62 | admission 5 euros | tram 1, 2, 5, 6, 7, 10 Leidseplein*

CINEMAS

All films are shown in the original language with Dutch subtitles. Evening screenings usually start at 8 and 10pm. Some cinemas interrupt the movie for a ten-minute break.

INSIDER TIP THE MOVIES ● (123 D2) *(𝄞 F2)*

Smaller than the Tuschinski and not as well known, but almost equally beautiful: Amsterdam's oldest cinema on Haarlemmerdijk was opened in 1912. The auditorium and café-restaurant have Art Deco interiors. *Haarlemmerdijk 161 | tel. 020 6 38 60 16 | tram 3 Haarlemmerplein*

TUSCHINSKI ★ (120 B6) *(𝄞 G4)*

When the King's mother Beatrix feels like going to the cinema, she selects

Do good dancers go to heaven? Club Paradiso occupies a former church

the Tuschinski. And it's a right royal treat, this movie palace built in 1921, an architectural gem in the Expressionist style. Taking a seat in its great auditorium or strolling through the foyer you feel transported back to bygone days. *Reguliersbreestraat 26 | tel. 0900 14 58 | tram 4, 9, 14 Rembrandtplein*

CONCERTS & BALLET

BEURS VAN BERLAGE (120 C2) (*ф G3*)
The magnificent building that once served as a stock exchange is a venue for concerts given by the Dutch Philharmonic Orchestra, the Dutch Opera Orchestra, the Chamber Orchestra and the Amsterdam Symphony Orchestra. *Damrak 243 | tel. 020 5 31 33 50 | www.beursvanberlage.nl | tram 4, 9, 16, 24, 25 Dam*

CONCERTGEBOUW ⭐ (127 E3) (*ф E6*)
Amsterdam's concert hall is a legend, and so are its acoustics. In the box-like Main Hall with its restrained decoration you can hear a pin drop on the stage.
The Concertgebouworkest of the Netherlands capital is one of the world's finest orchestras and has a particularly strong tradition of performing Mahler and Bruckner. Free ● INSIDER TIP lunchtime concerts are held from September to May on Wednesdays at 12.30pm in the Recital Hall. *Concertgebouwplein 2–6 | tel. 0900 6 71 83 45 | www.concertgebouw.nl | tram 3, 5, 12, 16 Concertgebouw*

BOOKS & FILMS

▶ **Amsterdam. The Brief Life of a City** – If you want to immerse yourself in the history of Amsterdam, this entertaining work (Geert Mak, 1999, also available as an e-book) is just the ticket.

▶ **Max Havelaar** – This anticolonial novel by Multatuli (alias Eduard Douwes Dekker) is a classic of Dutch literature. Written in 1860, it is set in Amsterdam and Indonesia.

▶ **The Assault** – Harry Mulisch (1982, a great name in modern Dutch literature, died 2010) set several stories in Amsterdam. This one takes place during the period of German occupation in the Second World War.

▶ **Amsterdamned** – This black thriller by Dick Maas (1988) is about a mysterious serial murderer who hides in the Amsterdam canal network. It includes a memorable speedboat chase.

▶ **The Discovery of Heaven** – Film version (2001, by Dutch director Jeroen Krabbé) of Harry Mulisch's bestseller. Most of it is set in the historic quarter of Amsterdam, and most of the roles are taken by British actors, including Stephen Fry.

▶ **Dutch Light** – Wonderful, award-winning documentation by Pieter-Rim de Kroons (2003) about the special quality of light on Dutch Old Master paintings. It shows many works from the Rijksmuseum, landscapes in and around Amsterdam and interviews with museum directors and artists.

When the ex-Queen goes to the movies, then only the Tuschinski will do

MUZIEKGEBOUW AAN 'T IJ

(124 B3) *(ⓜ H3)*

The concerts in the two halls of this glass palace on the water are usually devoted to contemporary music. The walls, ceiling and floor of the larger hall are movable so that the acoustics can be perfectly tuned to every kind of music. *Piet Heinkade 1 | www.muziekgebouw. nl | tram 25, 26 Muziekgebouw*

HET MUZIEKTHEATER ★

(121 D5) *(ⓜ G4)*

When it was opened in 1986 this forbidding-looking modern complex on Waterlooplein was controversial. Meanwhile the people of Amsterdam have accepted it, as it gave them not only a new city hall but also the only opera house in the Netherlands. Their name for the monumental edifice is *Stopera,* fusing Stadhuis (city hall) and opera. In the Boekmanzaal, INSIDER TIP free lunchtime concerts are held on Tuesdays at 12.30pm. *Waterlooplein 22 | tel. 020 6 25 54 55 | tram 9, 14 Waterlooplein*

THEATRE

INSIDER TIP BOOM CHICAGO

(127 F1) *(ⓜ E5)*

Boom Chicago stages an extremely entertaining comedy programme and improvisational theatre in English, with the option of combining the performance with a (generally mediocre) meal. In the *Rozentheater | Rozengracht 117 | tel. 020 4 23 01 01 | www. boomchicago.nl | tram 10, 13, 14, 17 Marnixstraat/Rozengracht*

STADSSCHOUWBURG ★

(127 F1) *(ⓜ E5)*

In 1894 the municipal theatre opened on Leidseplein with an ornate Neorenaissance façade. Its stage is the scene for major productions of classic drama such as works by Ibsen and Chekhov but also for contemporary experimental theatre. In summer much of the Holland Festival takes place here. *Leidseplein 26 | tel. 020 6 24 23 11 | tram 1, 2, 5, 6, 7, 10, 17 Leidseplein*

WHERE TO STAY

Although there are approximately 375 hotels with 48,000 beds in Amsterdam, it's not easy to find a good room at a reasonable price. The city boasts 10 million overnight stays per year. Prices are high, standards are not; a double room, even in a basic hotel is hard to find for less than 120 euros.

If style and atmosphere matter to you, then you'll have to pay more – and often book incredibly early. On no account should you arrive without a room reservation! In the peak season (Easter to October) hotels and guesthouses in all price categories are often booked out months in advance.

However, amongst Amsterdam's hotels there are also a few real gems. They include big, luxury hotels with a long tradition and guesthouses hidden away in crooked buildings on canals. The latter often have bags of charm, but that comes with the odd drawback: alarmingly steep stairs and draughty windows are not uncommon. One thing to watch out for is that many small hotels don't take credit cards! Value added tax is included in the price, breakfast too from the medium price category upwards. If you arrive by car, don't fail to ask about parking facilities when you book. Parking on the street is very expensive in the city centre, especially if you fail to buy a ticket and get landed with a fine. Hotels without their own parking spaces sometimes have permits for guests or special deals with local car parks. You

Photo: Conservatory of the Grand Hotel Krasnapolsky

Modern on the waterfront, gently rocking on a canal or traditional style in the centre: in Amsterdam rooms are not cheap but they have charm

can book a hotel room online at *www.hotels.nl* or directly with *Iamsterdam*, *www.iamsterdam.com*. If you fancy a night on the water, search *www.houseboathotel.nl* for INSIDER TIP ► accomodation on houseboats.

HOTELS: EXPENSIVE

AMERICAN HOTEL (127 F1) (*ⓜ E5*)
A wonderful Art Nouveau building. Although the rooms have been modernised, some of the old-fashioned leaded-light

windows remain. Don't miss the Grand Café on the ground floor. *188 rooms | Leidsekade 97 | tel. 020 5 56 30 00 | www.edenamsterdamamericanhotel. com | tram 1, 2, 5, 6, 7, 10 Leidseplein*

COLLEGE HOTEL (127 F3) (*ⓜ F7*)
The Amsterdam school of hotel management operates this luxurious boutique hotel in an attractive 19th-century school building near Museumplein. Spacious rooms, friendly staff. *40 rooms | Roelof Hartstraat 1 | tel. 020*

Anouska Hempel, has gone to town with opulent striped fabrics and dark colours – she knows no taboos, not even walls painted black. Guests have the choice between seven different styles of room, from classic and antique to Asian and minimalist. *41 rooms | Keizersgracht 384 | tel. 020 5 30 20 10 | www.dylan amsterdam.com | tram 13, 14, 17 Raad-huisstraat*

ESTHERÉA (120 A4) (*F4*)

This third-generation family-run business is run in a total of six converted canal-side houses. In the most recent refurbishment the 1930s style was fortunately kept. *70 rooms | Singel 303–309 | tel. 020 6 24 51 46 | www.estherea.nl | tram 13, 14, 17 Raadhuisstraat*

GRAND HOTEL AMRÂTH AMSTERDAM (124 A4) (*H3*)

The Amrâth Hotel opened in 2007 in the imposing early 20th-century Scheepvaartgebouw. The foyer and staircase were restored according to the original design, and the Art Deco style of the building guided the furnishing of the large, high-ceilinged rooms. *165 rooms | Prins Hendrikkade 108 | 10 min. on foot from the main station | tel. 020 5 52 00 00 | www.amrathamster dam.nl*

NH GRAND HOTEL KRASNAPOLSKY (120 B3) (*F3*)

Indisputably the 'grande dame' of Amsterdam's hotels. Breakfast and lunch are served in the centrepiece of this imposing Neoclassical building on the Dam: the superb INSIDER TIP conserva-tory with its glass dome, a protected architectural feature. Gustav Mahler once breakfasted here. *469 rooms | Dam 9 | tel. 020 5 54 91 11 | www.nh-hotels.com | tram 13, 14, 16, 24, 25 Dam*

Hotel Pulitzer: over 200 rooms in 24 houses on the canals

5 71 15 11 | www.thecollegehotel.com | tram 3, 5, 12, 24, 25 Roelof Hartplein

THE DYLAN ⭐ (123 D5) (*F4*)

An upmarket design hotel in a 17th-century canal house. The owner, designer

MÖVENPICK AMSTERDAM
(124 B4) (*ⅅ H3*)

The Mövenpick Hotel with its 408 stylish and modern rooms occupies a striking high-rise on the IJ. If you book a room 🌿 as high up as possible on the west side, you will have a terrific view across the water and the city! *Piet Heinkade 11 | tel. 020 519 12 00 | www. moevenpick-hotels.com | tram 25, 26 Muziekgebouw*

OKURA
(128 B4) (*ⅅ F7*)

A little bit of Japan in Amsterdam. This luxury hotel in the lively De Pijp quarter has everything needed to soothe a weary guest – above all, the service is perfect. The 321 rooms have been lavishly fitted out on a generous scale. The architects had a nice idea: the lighting on the roof of this conspicuous skyscraper acts as a barometer. If the lights glow blue, the weather will be good. *Ferdinand Bolstraat 333 | tel. 020 678 71 11 | www.okura.nl | tram 24, 25 Jozef Israëlskade*

PULITZER ★ (123 D5) (*ⅅ F4*)

This hotel complex consists of no less than 24 (!) canal houses dating from the 17th and 18th centuries with 224 individually furnished rooms. Winding corridors and the secluded garden add to the historic atmosphere. *Prinsengracht 315–331 | tel. 020 523 52 35 | www.starwoodhotels. com | tram 13, 14, 17 Westermarkt*

HOTELS: MODERATE

ARENA ★ (129 D2) (*ⅅ J5*)

Hotel with minimalist styling aiming at a young clientele in what was once an orphanage. Some of the rooms are across two levels. *116 rooms | s'Gravesandestraat 51 | tel. 020 8 50 24 00 | www.hotelarena. nl | tram 6, 7, 10 s'Gravesandestraat*

CANAL HOUSE ★ (123 E4) (*ⅅ F3*)

Its American owner has combined two 17th-century canalside houses to create this stylish accommodation. All rooms have lovely old wooden floors, none have a TV. The breakfast room gives onto an overgrown garden. *23 rooms | Keizersgracht 148 | tel. 020 622 51 82 | www.canal house.nl | tram 13, 14, 17 Westermarkt*

CONSCIOUS HOTEL VONDELPARK ☺
(126 C2) (*ⅅ C6*)

One of Amsterdam's first true eco-hotels, at the southern end of Vondelpark. It consumes 20 per cent less energy than comparable accommodation, uses only biodegrad-

★ **The Dylan**
Design hotel with sumptuous decoration → p. 86

★ **Pulitzer**
24 canal houses and a pretty courtyard → p. 87

★ **Arena**
Minimalist design and trendy guests in a former orphanage → p. 87

★ **Canal House**
A hotel with lots of atmosphere, thanks to antiques and a wild garden → p. 87

★ **Amstel Botel**
Reasonably priced hotel boat → p. 91

★ **Citizen M**
Self-service design hotel at a budget price → p. 91

MARCO POLO HIGHLIGHTS

able cleaning materials, and puts fair-trade products on the breakfast table. *81 rooms | Overtoom 519 | tel. 020 8 20 33 33 | www.consciousho tels.com | tram 1 Overtoomsesluis*

DE FILOSOOF (127 D2) (*ØJ D5*)
Hotel in a quiet street near Vondelpark. Every room is dedicated to a philosopher or writer: the Aristotle room is Greek-inspired, and the walls of the Goethe room are adorned with quotes from Faust. *28 rooms | Anna van den Vondelstraat 6 | tel.*

020 6 83 30 13 | www.hotelfilosoof.nl | tram 1, 6 Overtoom

HOTEL V FREDERIKSPLEIN
(128 B2) (*ØJ G6*)
Design hotel located on the southern edge of the old quarter. Relatively small rooms, but they are equipped with flatscreen TVs and comfortable beds. The lobby is more like a lounge bar – and it even has a fireplace. *48 rooms | Weter-ingschans 136 | tel. 020 6 62 32 33 | www. hotelv.nl | tram 7, 10, 25 Frederiksplein*

LUXURY HOTELS

Amstel Intercontinental
(128 C2) (*ØJ H5*)
A legendary high-class hotel built in 1867 in a delightful location on the Amstel (with winter garden). Crystal chandeliers and white marble are the hallmark of the lobbies, and the 79 suites (this is a suites-only hotel) are fitted out according to guests' wishes. The gym and starred restaurant are also open to non-residents. *From 425 euros | Professor Tulpplein 1 | tel. 020 6 22 60 60 | amsterdam.interconti.com | Metro Wibautstraat*

Conservatorium Hotel (127 E2) (*ØJ E6*)
The former conservatorium along the Museumplein now is an exclusive de-signer hotel, furnished by the Ital-ian designer Piero Lissoni. On offer are an extensive spa, but also an ar-cade filled with nobel boutiques, the highly praised restaurant *Tunes* as well as a brasserie. *129 rooms | Van Baer-lestraat 27 | tel. 020 5 70 00 00 | www. conservatoriumhotel.com | tram 2, 3, 5, 12 Van Baerlestraat*

The Grand Amsterdam (120 C4) (*ØJ G4*)
The 14th-century building has served in its time as a monastery, princely court, seat of the admiralty and town hall. Now it's a luxury hotel with marble floors, precious tapestries on the walls and Art Nouveau wallpaper. *Double from approx. 425 euros | 138 rooms | Oudezijds Voorburgwal 197 | tel. 020 5 55 31 11 | www.thegrand.nl | tram 4, 9, 16, 24, 25 Dam*

Hotel de l'Europe (120 B5) (*ØJ G4*)
Late 19th-century building furnished in a style of restrained elegance. The location between Amstel, Singel and Kloveniersburgwal is as good as it gets. The rooms facing the city have warm, dark colours, those looking out to the river have a lighter colour scheme and French windows. *From 270 to 350 euros | 183 rooms | Nieuwe Doelenstraat 2–8 | tel. 020 5 311 77 | www.leurope.nl |tram 4, 9, 14, 16, 24, 25 Muntplein*

IBIS AMSTERDAM STOPERA
(121 E4) (*🛱 H4*)

This branch of the large chain is situated near the maritime museum. It's a good bet if you arrive by car, as there are parking spaces (if not free of charge) in a nearby car park. *207 rooms | Valkenburgerstraat 68 | tel. 020 531 91 35 | Metro Waterlooplein*

INSIDER TIP LLOYD HOTEL
(125 D4) (*🛱 K3*)

Art and design hotel in a magnificent building on the eastern harbour islands that was once a hostel for people emigrating with the Lloyd shipping line. 116 individually furnished rooms. *Oostelijke Handelskade 34 | tel. 020 561 36 36 | www.lloydhotel.com | tram 10 C. van Eesterenlaan*

RÉSIDENCE LE COIN (120 B5) (*🛱 G4*)

This place used to provide an overnight stay for guests of the University of Amsterdam, but its seven historic buildings are now available to all. The rooms are basically small apartments with a kitchenette and their own doorbell. *42 rooms | Nieuwe Doelenstraat 5 | tel. 020 524 68 00 | www.lecoin.nl | tram 4, 9, 14, 16, 24, 25 Muntplein*

RHO (120 B3) (*🛱 G4*)

Pleasant little hotel in a quiet side street off the Dam. The building was previously a theatre, and the former stage is now a common room and breakfast room. *105 rooms | Nes 5–23 | tel. 020 620 73 71 | www.rhohotel.com | tram 4, 9, 16, 24, 25 Dam*

NH SCHILLER (120 C6) (*🛱 G5*)

'The best hotelier who paints, and the best painter who runs a hotel' – thus was Frits Schiller described in his own lifetime. He decorated the walls of his hotel,

Is design your thing? The colourful lobby of the Lloyd Hotel

which was founded in 1912, by painting murals. In the 1920s Schiller's hotel was a meeting place for artists. Today this Art Deco building is also popular because of its central location on Rembrandtplein. *92 rooms | Rembrandtplein 26–36 | tel. 020 554 07 77 | www.nh-hotels.com | tram 4, 9, 14 Rembrandtplein*

SEVEN BRIDGES (128 B1) (*🛱 G5*)

You really can see seven canal bridges from this hotel. Each room is individually furnished, all of them with antiques and art. Ask for the INSIDER TIP room with a fireplace! *11 rooms | Reguliersgracht 31 | tel. 020 6 23 13 29 | www.sevenbridges hotel.nl | tram 4, 6, 7, 10 Frederiksplein*

LOW BUDGET

▶ *Cocomama* **(128 B2)** *(יִ G2) (from approx. 30 euros for a 6-bed room; approx. 50 euros for a double room | Westeinde 18 | tel. 020 6 27 24 54 | www.cocomama.nl | Tram 4, 7, 10, 25 Frederiksplein)* is the first 'Boutique-Hostel' in Amsterdam: opened in 2010 it combines authentic, beautifully decorated rooms with the sociability of a hostel – tomcat Joop also belongs to it.

▶ The website *www.bedandbreak fast.nl* is where to look for the biggest range of bed & breakfast houses in Amsterdam. *From approx. 20 euros/person*

▶ *Bob's Youth Hostel (dorm bed from 14 euros |* **(120 B2)** *(יִ G3) Nieuwezijds Voorburgwal 92 | tel. 020 6 23 00 63 | tram 1, 2, 5, 13, 17 Dam)* is in the heart of the city. It's a stopping-off place for backpackers from all over the world and has a pleasant, relaxed atmosphere.

▶ The *Bicycle Hotel (double 50–80 euros |* **(128 B3)** *(יִ G7) Van Ostadestraat 123 | tel. 020 6 79 34 52 | www.bicyclehotel.com | tram 24, 25 Albert Cuypstraat)* is a guest house with bike hire in De Pijp. 17 rooms, clean but a bit on the small side, and a nice breakfast room.

TOREN (123 E4) *(יִ F3)*
Hotel by the Westerkerk, run by the same family for generations. The 40 rooms are divided between two 17th-century canal houses. Nice garden. *Keizersgracht 164 | tel. 020 6 22 60 33 | www.toren.nl | tram 13, 14, 17 Westermarkt*

WIECHMANN (123 D5) *(יִ F3)*
Hotel in an ideal location occupying several restored buildings on a canal. 40 rooms decorated in a modern or antique style, as well as family rooms. *Prinsengracht 328–332 | tel. 020 6 26 33 21 | www.hotelwiechmann.nl | tram 13, 14, 17 Westermarkt*

HOTEL SPA ZUIVER ● (0) *(יִ 0)*
This spa hotel on the edge of the *Amsterdamse Bos* woods is just right if you want peace and natural surroundings. The room price includes use of the pool, sauna and gym. The metro takes you to the centre of Amsterdam in 15 minutes. *31 rooms | Koenenkade 8 | tel. 020 3 01 07 10 | www.spazuiver.nl | Metro 51 A. J. Ernststraat*

HOTELS: BUDGET

AALDERS (127 F2) *(יִ E5)*
Lively little hotel fitted out in a functional modern way near Museumplein. Spacious rooms with large windows; breakfast is served in an attractive room on the 2nd floor. *28 rooms | Jan Luykenstraat 1–15 | tel. 020 6 73 40 27 | www.hotelaalders.nl | tram 2, 5 Hobbemakade*

ACACIA (123 D3) *(יִ E2)*
Plain and clean hotel in the Jordaan district with a view of Lijnbaansgracht. *20 rooms | Lindengracht 251 | tel. 020 6 22 14 60 | www.hotelacacia.nl | tram 3 Marnixplein*

AMSTEL BOTEL ⭐ (121 E2) (*◫ 0*)
The crossing on the free ferry from the main station to a former shipyard in the Noord district takes only 10 minutes. A semi-abandoned dock area, where there are just a few restaurants and studios is the mooring site of the Botel hotel ship with its 174 cabins. Come here if you like a harbour and artists' milieu. *Tel. 020 6 26 42 47 | www.amstelbotel.nl*

ARMADA (128 B1) (*◫ G5*)
Probably the cheapest overnight stay on Amsterdam's fancy Keizersgracht. Not all the rooms have en-suite bathrooms. *26 rooms | Keizersgracht 713–715 | tel. 020 6 23 29 80 | tram 4 Keizersgracht*

CITIZEN M ⭐ (127 E5) (*◫ E8*)
Budget design hotel in the south of the city. The tiny but very stylish rooms have king-size beds, LCD televisions and tropical-rain showers. The ground-floor lounges too have designer furnishings. There is no reception, and has a self-service bar instead of a restaurant. *215 rooms | Prinses Irenestraat 30 | tel. 020 8 11 70 90 | www.citizenm.com | tram 5 Prinses Irenestraat | Metro 50, 51: Zuid WTC*

EUPHEMIA (128 B2) (*◫ F5*)
Hotel in a former monastery near Leidseplein. Relaxed atmosphere, plain and good-value rooms. *15 rooms | Fokke Simonszstraat 1–9 | tel. 020 6 22 90 45 | www.euphemiahotel.com | tram 16, 24, 25 Weteringscircuit*

MUSEUMZICHT
(127 F2) (*◫ F5*)
The name tells you what you get: a view of the Rijksmuseum opposite. The owner used to be an antiques dealer, which is why every corner of the breakfast room is

crammed full. Take care on the extremely steep stairs! *14 rooms | Jan Luykenstraat 22 | tel. 020 6 71 29 54 | tram 2, 5 Hobbemastraat*

Let the waves rock you to sleep: Amstel Botel

PARKZICHT (127 E2) (*◫ E5*)
Small hotel in a quiet side street off Vondelpark. Old Dutch furniture in dark wood. Some double rooms have a good view of the park. *14 rooms | Roemer Visscherstraat 33 | tel. 020 6 18 19 54 | www.parkzicht.nl | tram 2, 3, 5, 12 Overtoom*

ST CHRISTOPHER'S INN
(120 C3) (*◫ G3*)
At the heart of the red-light district. The hotel bar and discotheque *Winston Kingdom* are not only for residents. Most of the 67 rooms were styled by artists and

designers, and even the ground-floor toilet is a miniature gallery. *Warmoesstraat 123–129 | 10 min. on foot from the main station | tel. 020 6 23 13 80 | www.st-christophers.co.uk/amsterdamhostels*

PRIVATE ACCOMMODATION

B28 (120 B1) (*魚 F3*)
A historic sailing ship has found a new role as a B & B on Herengracht, providing accommodation for two in the heart of Amsterdam. *Herengracht 28 G | tel. 06 29 03 59 56 | www.b28.nl | 5 min. on foot from the main station | budget*

BED & BREAKFAST BOVEN IJ
(124 C1) (*魚 K1*)
This pretty double room in an old dyke house in Amsterdam-Noord, with the added bonus of free parking, is ideal for drivers. The bus and ferry take you to the city centre in only 10 minutes. *Leeuwarderweg 50 | tel. 020 4 21 89 56 | www.bbbovenij.nl | bus 32, 33, 38 Merelstraat | Budget*

THE FLYING PANCAKE (128 C1) (*魚 H5*)
Upmarket bed & breakfast with two suites in an 18th-century house, where designer washbasins meet antique furniture. *Nieuwe Kerkstraat 15 | tel. 06 38 30 52 19 | www.theflyingpancake. com | Metro Waterlooplein | Moderate*

INSIDER TIP ▶ LEVANT B & B
(125 E4) (*魚 L3*)
It would be hard to find accommodation more typical of Amsterdam than this old barge in the eastern harbour district. The large cabin is fitted out for two guests and has its own bathroom. *Levantkade 90 | www.levantbb.nl | tram 10 Azartplein | Moderate*

MIAUW SUITES (123 E5) (*魚 F3*)
Two bright, 70-square-metre apartments with living room, bedroom and kitchen facilities, tastefully furnished with design items. *Hartenstraat 3 | tel. 020 7 17 34 29 | www.miauw.com | tram 13, 14, 17 Westermarkt | Expensive*

MS LUCTOR ☺ (123 E2) (*魚 F1*)
Bed & breakfast with three attractive cabins in an old barge in the Westerdok harbour basin near the main station. The ship is powered by solar energy, and guests can undertake environmentally sound trips around the city by bicycle or canoe. *Westerdok 103 | tel. 06 22 68 95 06 | www.boatbedandbreakfast.nl | bus 48 Barentszplein | Moderate*

B & B SILODAM ☙ (123 E1) (*魚 F1*)
65-square-metre apartment in an old silo building with a view of the timber dock. *Silodam 129 | tel. 06 34 30 30 38 | www.bb-silodam.nl | bus 48 Barentszplein | Budget*

STUDIO INN (123 E1) (*魚 F1*)
A view of the Westerdok is given from the two well lit doublerooms of the *Studio Inn*. The big room provides a fridge and a dining table, on which local organic products are served for breakfast. If you are traveling in a group of four, you can additionally rent the smaller room next door. *Barentszplein 3 | tel. 06 14 77 68 65 | www.studio-inn.nl | bus 48 Barentszplein | Budget*

SUITE 2 STAY (128 B2) (*魚 G5*)
Two holiday apartments in a quiet street at the edge of the historic quarter. The ground-floor studio is modern and simply styled, while the one on the first floor has neo-Baroque furnishings. Both of them sleep two to three people. *Fokke*

WHERE TO STAY

Simonszstraat 76 A-1 | tel. 06 10 01 46 41 | www.amsterdamsuitestay.com | tram 4, 7, 10, 16, 24, 25 Weteringcircuit | Budget

HOSTELS

STAYOKAY STADSDOELEN (120 C5) (*Ø G4*)
This is a relatively small hostel near Waterlooplein. Not suitable for groups. Beds from 19 euros. *170 beds | Kloveniersburgwal 97 | tel. 020 6 24 68 32 | www.stayokay.com | tram 4, 9, 16, 24, 25 Muntplein*

STAYOKAY VONDELPARK (127 E2) (*Ø E5*)
The big plus with this hostel is its top location: a large villa situated directly by Vondelpark. Bed approx. 19 euros. *500 beds | Zandpad 5 | tel. 020 5 89 89 99 | www.stayokay.com | tram 1, 2, 5, 6, 7, 10 Leidseplein*

CAMPING

CAMPING VLIEGENBOS (125 D1) (*Ø K1*)
This is an option if you are on a tight budget. North of the IJ, it is the nearest camp site to the city. Free ferry to the main station. From 7.60 euros per person, 8 euros per car. *April–Sept | Meeuwenlaan 138 | tel. 020 6 36 88 55 | www.vliegenbos.com | bus 38, 39 Meeuwenlaan*

CAMPING ZEEBURG (0) (*Ø 0*)
This year-round campsite lies on an island in the IJmeer to the east of Amsterdam. You can rent a INSIDER TIP colourful little caravan or a cabin. The nearest tram stop is about 10 min. away on foot. From 6.50 euros per person, 4 euros per car. *Zuider IJdijk 20 | tel. 020 6 23 28 18 | www.campingzeeburg.nl | tram 26 Zuiderzeeweg*

B & B Silodam in an old brick-built warehouse: a spectacular location on the water with a view of the timber dock

WALKING TOURS

The tours are marked in green in the street atlas,
the pull-out map and on the back cover

1 DISCOVERING THE COURTYARDS OF JORDAAN

Behind many an inconspicuous door in Amsterdam there is a little hidden world: a *hofje* (courtyard). If you boldly enter, you will find a tiny, village-like courtyard surrounded usually by crooked houses und lovingly tended front gardens. On this two-and-a-half-hour walk around ★ *Jordaan*, a quarter built for the common people, you can explore a few of these secret spots.

Hofjes are not only found in Jordaan. The best-known one, the Begijnhof → p. 30, lies at the heart of Amsterdam's city centre. But nowhere else have so many residential courtyards survived as in Jordaan, which was once a district of the poor. The yards were originally donated by rich merchants as dwellings for the old or poor, so that people in need could have free accommodation. Today these green havens are mostly occupied by rented flats. From Monday to Friday *hofjes* are generally accessible between 10am and 5pm. Have the heart to do so, but do be considerate, and refrain from encroaching on the residents' privacy!

This tour starts in Elandsstraat. To get there, catch tram no. 6, 10 or 17. At number 104–142, a 19th-century building at the entrance conceals the Venetiaehofje, which was founded in 1650. The donor of this courtyard, Jacob Stoffels, had made his fortune trading with Venice. Grouped around an overgrown little garden with

---

Photo: New architecture on the island of the Royal Netherlands Steamship Company

Between backyards and harbour islands:
Amsterdam is a fantastic place for
walking around

an old lantern are low houses, accommodation originally for poor widows and 'old spinsters', and later for Huguenots who had fled from France.

A passage takes you through the house at the back, dating from 1904, and onto Lauriergracht, a canal that connects with Prinsengracht exactly at the place where, on the opposite side of the canal, you will find the Nieuwe Suykerhofje (Prinsengracht 385–393) – although from outside you would never guess it's there. The front door on the right of a fine patri-

cian's house turns out to be the entrance to a narrow alley where you come upon a gate. Beyond it is a tiny hofje that was established for Catholic widows in 1755 by a rich confectioner. Six small three-storey houses and a chapel are grouped around a narrow, paved open space. Because of the lack of space, the widows lived one above the other here: there are two cramped apartments on each floor. Continue along Prinsengracht and through a few typical, picturesque Jordaan lanes into Egelantiersgracht. Here, don't miss the `INSIDER TIP` *Sint Andrie-shofje*. Founded in 1614, it is the oldest *hofje* in Amsterdam after the Begijnhof. You can recognise it, like most other courtyards, by the long row of house numbers at the gateway: 105–141. The blue-and-white Delft tiles at the entrance to this secluded idyll are truly lovely. Behind it is a nicely kept garden with an 18th-century water pump. A further courtyard is tucked away at 1e Egelan-tiersdwarsstraat 1–5; today it is used for student accommodation. A good place to take a break on the way there is ● `INSIDER TIP` *Café 't Smalle* on the corner of Prinsengracht. It still has its original wooden interior dating from 1780. Continue through 2e Tuindwarsstraat into *Tichelstraat* and on to Karthuizer-straat. Behind the uniform brick façade of no. 21–131 lies Karthuizerhof, an unexpectedly beautiful and large *hofje* with two old wells and tall trees. Before 1650 the Carthusian monastery that gave the courtyard its name stood here. It is the only *hofje* that was not paid for by a private donor, but was built by the city authorities as a kind of home for single mothers.

From here Lindenstraat takes you to the Noorderkerk, which catered to the spiritual needs of the Protestant residents of Jordaan. Most of the Catholic *hofjes* had a chapel of their own. An example of these is the Van Brienenhofje at Prinsengracht 85–133. Not built until 1804, it is one of the more recent courtyards, and very large. The main entrance, above which two putti hold a coat of arms with a cross, was reserved for the comings and goings of the regents, the supervisors of the community that lived here. They lived in the building at the entrance, which also housed the chapel and quarters for the porter. Today this high-class *hofje* is the abode of elderly Catholic ladies.

Walk along pretty *Brouwersgracht* onto Palmgracht, now no longer a canal, where one last *hofje* can be visited. You can identify it by means of a gable stone depicting a turnip above the archway. The cute Raepenhofje beyond it was established in 1648 by its patron Pieter Adriaensz Raep (enter next door through the door of the *Bossche Hofje*). According to tradition Raep made his donation in thanks for the signing of the Peace of Westphalia, but it is more probable that, like most of the donors of a *hofje*, his intention was to ensure the peace of his own soul. The walk ends here, at the northern tip of the Jordaan quarter. Tram no. 10 from Nassaukade will take you back to where you started.

2 A WALK AROUND THE WESTERN HARBOUR ISLANDS

One of Amsterdam's most attractive little-known areas lies close to the city centre. The islands that formed part of the former docks to the west of the centre still have their maritime atmosphere: historic warehouses, rusty cranes, workshop sheds and picturesque wooden bridges all form part of the scene. Duration of the walk: approx. 1.5 hours

The three harbour islands were built in the early 17th century at the same time as the Canal Ring. Originally they were the site of all industrial activities that produced too much noise or smell for the genteel parts of the city centre. Tar and salt making, rope manufacture, shipyards and fish processing operations all moved to the waterfront. Behind them warehouses, and before long residential buildings too for workers and sailors, were constructed. Nowadays almost all the old workshops have been converted into apartments and artists' studios, and are coveted properties.

The courtyards in Jordaan help to lend this quarter its down-to-earth atmosphere

The islands can be reached from Haarlemmerdijk. Pass beneath the railway viaduct, and you are standing by the modern harbour basin of Westerdok. Then go along Blokmakerstraat and Hendrik Jonkerplein to reach **Bickersgracht**. Old brick houses, cobblestones and overgrown canalside gardens give this street its old-fashioned charm. It is difficult to imagine that this area was one of the least salubrious residential districts of the city in the 1960s.

The terrain on the other side of the canal is **Prinseneiland**, which is accessed by crossing a bridge. **Galgenstraat** (gallows road) is the name of the lane beyond it, as this was once the way to the site of the gallows on the northern bank of the river IJ. There is nothing morbid, however, about the handsome warehouses that line the entire island. Their names – De Windhond (greyhound), De Teerton (tar barrel) or De Witte Pelicaan (the white pelican) – are illustrated by pretty gable stones or written in looping letters on the window shutters.

Cross the bridge named **Drieharingen-brug** to get to the **Realeneiland**. The attractive drawbridge got its name from a house on the other side of the canal named 'De drie Haringen' (the three herrings). To this day a gable stone above the door bears witness to the fact that a ship's carpenter called Haring Booy built it. A good number of barges that have been converted to houseboats are moored on **Realengracht**, the banks of which are lined by little shipyard workshops. The quay round the corner is called INSIDER TIP *Kai Zandhoek* after the sand market that was established there in 1634. The sand merchants unloaded their cargo right in front of the houses, and a row of fine canal houses remains as testimony to the wealth of some of the merchants who lived here. A pleasant **café-restaurant → p. 63** has opened in the last house in the row, the **Gouden Reael**.

By walking along Bickersgracht you can return to Hendrik Jonkerplein, then under the railway viaduct go back to

Haarlemmerdijk. To finish the trip you can browse in the shops here or drink a cup of coffee.

A WALK ON THE EASTERN HARBOUR ISLANDS

From the man-made islands Java, KNSM and Borneo-Sporenburg, ocean liners once set off for far-away places. When passenger voyages came to an end and harbour activities moved elsewhere, the islands became wasteland. They were rediscovered in the 1990s and have developed into a fashionable residential area for many young people, with a lot of experimental architecture but also some survivals from the days of the docks. This two-and-a-half-hour walk will give you some impressions of a trendy new quarter.

Since 2005 the new number 26 tram route has linked the islands to the main station. Get off at the Rietlandpark stop and walk between the imposing Lloyd Hotel → p. 89, built in 1918 to accommodate people emigrating with the shipping line of that name, and its former quarantine buildings to the IJ harbour. From here you have a good view of INSIDER TIP the islands and their contemporary architecture. Across the water you will see Java-eiland with its varied urban residential buildings and KNSM-eiland, where there is a mixture of large blocks of flats and pretty houseboats.

A walk across the islands on a sunny day reveals all the charm of this mixed development. Behind the white IJ Tower the zinc façade of the The Whale residential block glitters in the rays of the sun. Beyond it on the Sporenburg peninsula are low terraced houses made from dark brick. The architects found inventive solutions to cope with the requirements that the island should be densely built but with low buildings. The result was a new kind of house, turned inwards with roof terraces and inner courtyards. Apart from the pots of flowers and little benches in front of the houses there are no gardens – the water of the harbour basin is the substitute here for green spaces. Almost everyone who lives here has a little boat. Walk onto the expressively curved, bright red ⚓ bridge that leads across the Spoorwegbassin to Borneo island to survey the surroundings and get a look at the big tankers in the distance as they sail out towards the North Sea.

On the other side of the bridge is something unusual. In INSIDER TIP Scheepstimmermanstraat the municipality of Amsterdam sold building plots to private buyers for the first time since the 16th century – an exceptional event in the Netherlands. All purchasers were permit-

ted to have a detached house designed by an architect of their choice. Many of them opted for young architects, and the result is extremely varied: it's like taking a walk through a colourful gallery of architectural experiments. Two of the most remarkable houses are number 120, in which a tree is growing, and number 62, which is clad in wood all round.

A second red bridge, which was designed with cyclists in mind and is therefore lower, takes you back to the Walfisch (whale) building and from there across a causeway to KNSM, the island of the royal Dutch shipping line (Koninklijke Nederlandse Stoomboot-Maatschappij). It is dominated by a large, sculptural residential block called Piraeus, the work of German architects Kollhoff & Rapp, which has been constructed around a small older building. If you are ready by now to take a break, the recommended café is Kanis en Meiland in the Piraeus building. From the waterfront café terrace you can watch what is happening on the decks of the houseboats in the harbour.

To the west of the connecting causeway KNSM borders Java-eiland, where the atmosphere is more urban. On the north side of the island residential high-rises line the busy Sumatra quayside road. However, the inner part of the island is a lovely, quiet green space where only pedestrians and cyclists have access.

Now walk along the cobblestones of Javakade to the Jan Schaeffer Bridge. At the far side of this on Oostelijke Handelskade stands an old harbour building that has been converted into an arts centre. If you still have the energy for more walking, head along the fish-shaped cruise ship terminal and the Muziekgebouw back to the station. Otherwise take a tram from the Kattenburgerstraat stop.

Not everyone comes here for the contemporary architecture of the harbour islands

TRAVEL WITH KIDS

ARTIS ● (124 B6) (🚇 H4)

Visitors to the Amsterdam zoo can see 1400 species from all over the world. Native fauna is here too: all the animals in the petting zoo are from breeds of old Dutch domestic animals.

One of the aquariums is a real curiosity. It shows the INSIDER TIP microcosm of an Amsterdam canal, including dumped bikes and a wrecked car. *Nov–March 9am–5pm, April–Oct 9am–6pm | admission 19.50 euros, children under 9 15.95 euros | Plantage Kerklaan 38/40 | tram 9, 14 Plantage Kerklaan | www.artis.nl*

CANAL BIKE

You can explore the canals of Amsterdam on a conventional boat trip, but why not get some exercise and do it by pedalo? If the weather is bad, all intrepid young navigators will be equipped with a waterproof cape. The boats are moored by the Rijksmuseum *(127 F2) (🚇 F5) (Stadhouderskade 42)*, on *Leidseplein (127 E–F1) (🚇 E5)*, at the Anne Frank Huis *(123 D4) (🚇 F3) (Prinsengracht 42)* and on the corner of *Keizersgracht/Leidsestraat (123 D6) (🚇 F4)*. *8 euros per person per hour, for more than 2 persons 7 euros per person per hour | www.canal.nl*

CHILDREN'S FARMS

Every sizeable park in Amsterdam has a free children's farmyard where all kinds of animals, from pigs and cows to guinea pigs, can be admired, and some of them petted. e.g. *Overbrakerpad 10 (122 B1) (🚇 D1) | Tue–Sun 10am–5pm | tram 10 Van Hallstraat*

GOAT FARMYARD (0) (🚇 0)

In the middle of woodland in Amsterdam there is a farmyard full of goats. 150 goats and kids (the four-legged variety) roam here, and children can comb and milk them. On Saturdays there are demonstrations of how cheese is made from fresh goat's milk. *Wed–Mon 10am–5pm | free admission | Nieuwe Meerlaan 4 | bus 194 Schiphol Oost*

NEMO SCIENCE CENTER (121 F2) (🚇 H3)

This science museum is full of activities for kids. They can blow bubbles big enough to stand in, make their own liquorice or find out why you can see through water. Hands-on is the motto here. In summer there is a ● café with paddling pool on the roof. *Tue–Sun 10am–5pm | admission 12.50 euros, free for children up to 3 years old | Oosterdok*

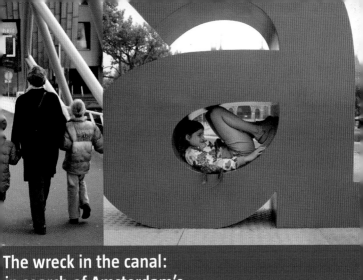

The wreck in the canal: in search of Amsterdam's underwater secrets

2 | 10 min. on foot from the main station | www.e-nemo.nl

PANNENKOEKENBOOT (0) (🛈 0)

Pancakes galor are offered in the *Pannekoekenboot*. While the little ones sprinkle crumble on their pancakes, mum and dad can peacefully enjoy the hour long round trip across the IJ, from the former wood harbour *(Houthaven)* to the main railway station and the easterly harbour islands. *Wed, Fri, Sat, Sun 4.30 and 6pm | adults 16 euros, children 3–12 ys. 11 euros | departure from NDSM-wharf (20 min. ride with the ferry from the main railway station) | www.pannen koekenboot.com*

RACE PLANET FOR KIDS (0) (🛈 0)

This indoor hall for karting, in the middle of an industrial district, is for kids only. Eight to sixteen-year-olds can zoom around here for all they're worth on two racetracks. Small-format versions of all manner of vehicles are available, from an overhead railway to an electric Formula One racing car. There is also a gigantic climbing frame and an enormous slide. *Mon, Tue, Thu 1–6pm, Wed noon–6pm, Fri noon–7pm, Sat 11am–7pm, Sun 11am–6pm | admission adults 3 euros, children up to 12 8.50 euros | Herwijk 10 | www.raceplanet.com | metro 50 to Sloterdijk, then bus 231, 233 Herwijk*

TUNFUN (121 E5) (🛈 H4)

Originally the plan was to build a road tunnel under the Mr. Visserplein. The project was abandoned when it was half completed. Instead it is now the site of the largest indoor playground in Amsterdam. Everything here is a bit bigger than usual: the toy construction site with three cranes, the maze, the slides and trampolines. There is even a children's hairdresser and a miniature cinema. *Daily 10am–6pm | free admission for adults, children up to the age of 12 8.50 euros | Mr. Visserplein 7 | tram 9, 14 Mr. Visserplein*

FESTIVALS & EVENTS

A wide range of different festivals and events are held in Amsterdam all year round, but especially in summer, when it's possible to celebrate outdoors on warm evenings with the canals as a magnificent backdrop. The Netherlands is not, however, one of those European countries with lots of public holidays: eight days a year is not many by international standards.

HOLIDAYS

1 Jan *Nieuwjaar*; **March/April** Good Friday; Easter Monday; **27 April** *Koningsdag*; **5 May** *Bevrijdingsdag, when only public institutions are closed;* **May/June** Ascension Day; Whit Monday; **25/26 Dec** *Christmas*

EVENTS

APRIL
▶ 27 April is ● ★ *Koningsdag.* Every year until 2013 the Dutch honoured their Queen on 30 April. With the coronation of Willem-Alexander this public holiday has been moved to his birthday on 27 April. For this occasion the whole of Amsterdam turns into one great flea market, and hordes of Dutch beer drinkers in orange t-shirts crowd the streets. A big open-air concert is held on Museumplein.

MAY
▶ *Bevrijdingsfestival:* Liberation from German occupation in the Second World War is commemorated on 5 May with an all-day open-air festival on Museumplein.

JUNE
▶ *Open Tuinen Dagen:* On the third weekend in June, 30 canal gardens open their doors to visitors.
▶ *Roots Festival:* Over ten days a colourful mixture of international world music bands performs at different places around the city. The festival concludes with a free open-air concert in Oosterpark.
▶ *Holland Festival:* A two-week event at which dance and theatre groups from all around the world make guest appearances in Amsterdam. The main venue is the Stadsschouwburg theatre on Leidseplein.
▶ Start of the INSIDER TIP ▶ *open-air season* in Vondelpark. Free performances of music and theatre until the end of August

In Amsterdam there's always a reason to celebrate. Preferably in summer and in a park, on a square or along a canal

JULY

▶ *Amsterdam Pride:* spectacular gay parade on the last weekend in July or the first weekend in August

AUGUST

▶ *De Parade:* Festival of theatre, music and more that moves between four Dutch cities. In Amsterdam it comes to Martin Luther King Park (early August).

▶ *Grachtenfestival:* The cultural highlight of the Amsterdam summer. The event that really draws the crowds is the free
▶ ★ *Prinsengrachtkonzert* in front of the Pulitzer Hotel in mid-August.

▶ ● *Pluk de Nacht:* Ten-day open-air film festival at the Stenen Hoofd on the bank of the IJ

SEPTEMBER

▶ *Jordaan Festival:* What started out as a neighbourhood party has developed into a large-scale fair with music and dancing

▶ *Open Monumentendag:* On the second Saturday of the month almost all historic monuments in the city are open.
▶ *Dutch Design Double:* Throughout September exhibitions and events connected with Dutch design are held at different locations in Amsterdam.

OCTOBER

▶ *Grachtenrace:* rowing regatta on the canals on the second Saturday of the month

NOVEMBER

On the third Sunday in November ▶ *Sinterklaas* (Santa Claus) arrives at the maritime museum by boat, mounts a horse there and rides on to the Dam.

DECEMBER

5 December is ▶ *Pakjesavond* (package eve). By tradition the Dutch give each other presents not at Christmas but on this day.

LINKS, BLOGS, APPS & MORE

LINKS

▶ www.spottedbylocals.com/amsterdam People who live in Amsterdam reveal their personal tips, from shops to restaurants and clubs. Lots of recommendations off the beaten track

▶ www.bookatable.com/nl/amsterdam/restaurants Many popular restaurants in Amsterdam are booked out weeks in advance. On this website you can check whether tables are available and reserve one online immediately

BLOGS & FORUMS

▶ www.amsterdamfoodie.nl/blog/ 'Restaurant reviews and decadent dining' is how an Amsterdam foodie from England, Vicky Hampton, describes her blog

▶ damstyle.blogspot.com What's the cool fashion at the moment in Amsterdam? This street-style photo blog shows you what to be seen in

▶ amsterdamize.com Marc van Woudenberg's blog in English is a collection of photos, videos and stories about cycling in 'the certified bicycle capital of the world'

VIDEOS & STREAMS

▶ www.amsterdamacoustics.com Films by international musicians who perform acoustic versions of their tracks on the streets in Amsterdam. Many of them are alternative bands, but a few better-known artists are among them

▶ www.youtube.com/watch?v=sTPsFlsxM3w Facts to counter prejudices: this likeable film defends the city of Amsterdam against claims that it is a hotbed of anarchists

Regardless of whether you are still preparing your trip or already in Amsterdam: these addresses will provide you with more information, videos and networks to make your holiday even more enjoyable

VIDEOS & STREAMS

▶ www.geobeats.com/videoclips/netherlands/amsterdam/jordaan An entertaining introduction to the Jordaan quarter, including courtyards, churches and the Anne Frank House

▶ www.youtube.com/watch?v=a09_wVSBkyw Amsterdam 100 years ago: not surprisingly, the biggest difference between this old footage and the urban scene today is the lack of cars on the streets

APPS

▶ GVB App This app by the city transportation company GVB tells you how to find the nearest tram stop wherever you may be, and when the next one will come along

▶ Spotted by Locals App Amsterdam If you have an iPhone, you can install the *Amsterdam Local Tips* to get ideas for seeing the sights and where to eat, leaving the tourist hordes behind

▶ UAR App For architecture fans this *Layar App UAR* has been produced by the *Arcam* centre for architecture to provide information on the spot about buildings in Amsterdam – and it even includes those that are yet to be built

NETWORKS

▶ www.facebook.com/21stcenturyvillage Facebook group all about new shops and the latest retail trends and tips in Amsterdam and London

▶ www.tripadvisor.co.uk/ShowForum-g188553-i58-The_Netherlands.html This well-known online forum gives you the opportunity to put all your questions about Amsterdam

▶ http://www.facebook.com/iamsterdam Facebook community of the city marketing organisation 'I amsterdam'. Visitors to Amsterdam can put their questions about what's on in the city and post photos, links that they like and other recommendations

▶ wiki.couchsurfing.org/en/Amsterdam A wiki entry on the couchsurfing network, which brings together people in different countries, and allows you to get to know or stay with people in Amsterdam

TRAVEL TIPS

ARRIVAL

Centraal Station has direct connections from major cities in western Europe, including high-speed Thalys links from Paris, Brussels and Cologne. From Britain, there are connections at Brussels with trains from London through the Channel Tunnel operated by Eurostar (tel: 08705 104 105; www.eurostar.com), with good-value through-fares to Amsterdam.

Amsterdam Schiphol Airport has excellent connections by scheduled flights to other European cities as well as intercontinental flights to North America. Typical flying times to Amsterdam: UK (1 hour), Dublin (1.5 hours), New York and Toronto (8 hours), Vancouver and Los Angeles (11 hours), Sydney (22 hours). Budget carriers such as BMIbaby, Flybe, EasyJet and Jet2 fly from British and Irish airports direct to Amsterdam. From Schiphol, about 11 miles southwest of the city, a train run every 15 minutes to the main station (journey time 20 min., fare 4 euros). A taxi to the city centre costs 45 euros. If you are staying in a 4- or 5-star hotel, the KLM shuttle bus will take you there, departing twice hourly. Schiphol: *tel. 0900 0141 | www.schiphol.nl*. If you find it easier to get a cheap flight to Rotterdam, then take bus 33 from Rotterdam airport to the station (20 minutes), from where trains take just under an hour to Amsterdam.

If you are driving, Amsterdam is easy to reach on the excellent Dutch motorway network, but congestion around and especially in the city mean this is not the recommended way to arrive. If you do drive, consider using the park and ride system, leaving your car at one of a number of points on the circular motorway A10: at Sloterdijk station, Zeeburgereiland, the Olympic stadium, Bos en Lommerplein and the Amsterdam Arena. For 8 euros per day (max. 4 days) you can park and also get five hourly tickets for public transportation. Give the ticket to the attendant so he can activate it for park and ride. *www.parkerenindestad.nl*

BICYCLE HIRE

Don't get into the saddle in Amsterdam unless you are used to cycling and feel confident, as the traffic is chaotic. But if you're up for it, a INSIDER TIP bike trip through the city is a memorable experience. Costs for bike hire start at 9 euros for 24 hours.
– ● *Star Bikes (De Ruyterkade 127 | tel. 020 6 20 32 15 | www.starbikesrental.com)*
– *Rent A Bike (Damstraat 20–22 | tel. 020 6 25 50 29 | www.bikes.nl)*

From arrival to weather

From the start to the end of the holiday:
useful addresses and information for your trip to Amsterdam

– Mac Bike (Weteringsschans 2, Leidseplein | Stationsplein 5 (main station) | Waterlooplein 199 | tel. 020 6 20 09 85 | www.macbike.nl)

CANAL TOURS

What would a trip to Amsterdam be without a canal tour? A number of companies run these tours, most of them starting from the main station or in front of the Rijksmuseum. In terms of their programme and prices there is little difference. Tickets can be purchased online, but usually you won't have to wait long if you just turn up, as the day-time tours start every 30 minutes. A one-hour trip takes you through the Canal Ring and Golden Arc, the Jordaan quarter, out onto the IJ, into the Oosterdok harbour basin and usually along a stretch of the Amstel. Recorded explanations are given in English and other languages. The price is about 13 euros (e.g. Rederij Lovers | www.lovers.nl | tel. 020 5 30 54 12; Amsterdam Canal Cruises | www.amsterdamcanalcruises.nl | tel. 020 6 26 56 36; Boathouse | tel. 020 3 37 97 33 | www.canalcruises amsterdam.com). Evening cruises with or without a meal are also on offer (see p. 80). Environmentally sound canal trips in ☺ gas-powered boats are operated by Amsterdam ECO Tours (120 C2) (𝝬 G3) (Damrak 6 | www.canal.nl | tel. 0900 3 33 44 42). If you want to take the helm yourself, hire a boat powered by green electricity from ☺ INSIDERTIP Boaty (128 B4) (𝝬 F7) (from 79 euros for 3 hours, max. 6 people | Ferdinand Bolstraat 333 | Tel. 06 27 14 94 93 | www.boaty.nl | tram 12, 25 Scheldestraat).

CONSULATES & EMBASSIES

BRITISH CONSULATE IN AMSTERDAM
Koningslaan 44 | tel. 020 6 76 43 43 | www.ukinnl.fco.gov.uk

CONSULATE OF THE USA IN AMSTERDAM
Museumplein 19 | tel. 020 5 75 53 30 | amsterdam.usconsulate.gov

CURRENCY CONVERTER

£	€	€	£
1	1.20	1	0.80
3	3.70	3	2.50
5	6.10	5	4.10
13	15.90	13	10.60
40	48.90	40	32.70
75	92	75	61
120	147	120	98
250	306	250	204
500	611	500	409

$	€	€	$
1	0.70	1	1.40
3	2.20	3	4.10
5	3.60	5	6.90
13	9.50	13	17.80
40	29.10	40	54.90
75	55	75	103
120	87	120	165
250	182	250	343
500	364	500	686

For current exchange rates see www.xe.com

CUSTOMS

Unlimited goods for personal use can be imported and exported without paying duties within states of the European Union. If you come from outside the EU, the duty-free allowances are: 1 litre of spirits or 2 litres of sparkling wine or 2 litres of fortified wine and 4 litres of non-sparkling wine; 200 cigarettes or 250 grammes of smoking tobacco or 100 cigarillos or 50 cigars, plus other goods with a maximum total value of 430 euros.

EMERGENCY

Ambulance, police, fire brigade: *tel. 112;* emergency doctor: *tel. 088 0 03 06 00*

EVENTS

The *Uitbureau (Leidseplein 26, in the Stadsschouwburg | Mon–Fri 10am–7.30 pm, Sat 10am–6pm, Sun noon–6pm | tram 1, 2, 5, 6, 7, 10)* sells tickets for all evening events. Telephone bookings (with credit card) in the Netherlands: *daily 9am–4pm | tel. 0900 0191 | on-line: www.aub.nl (only in Dutch).* From abroad: *tel. +31 2 06 211 2 88.* In the *Uitbureau* you can pick up the free monthly listings magazine *Uitkrant*. Another free Dutch publication with listings is *NL20*, which can be found at all sorts of places round the city. Information in English is published in the monthly *Time Out Magazine*, available from newsagents.

WEATHER IN AMSTERDAM

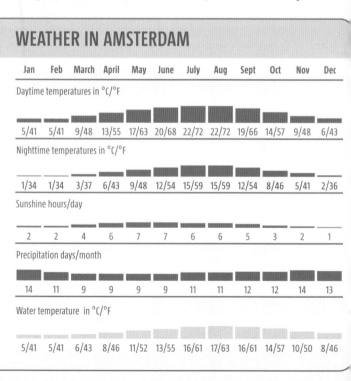

	Jan	Feb	March	April	May	June	July	Aug	Sept	Oct	Nov	Dec
Daytime temperatures in °C/°F	5/41	5/41	9/48	13/55	17/63	20/68	22/72	22/72	19/66	14/57	9/48	6/43
Nighttime temperatures in °C/°F	1/34	1/34	3/37	6/43	9/48	12/54	15/59	15/59	12/54	8/46	5/41	2/36
Sunshine hours/day	2	2	4	6	7	7	6	6	5	3	2	1
Precipitation days/month	14	11	9	9	9	9	11	11	12	12	14	13
Water temperature in °C/°F	5/41	5/41	6/43	8/46	11/52	13/55	16/61	17/63	16/61	14/57	10/50	8/46

GUIDED TOURS

Amsterdam is a good place to explore on foot. English-language tours through the historic districts are operated by big travel agencies and by companies such as *Local Experts (tel. 020 4 08 51 00 | www.local-experts.com)* and *TopTours (tel. 020 6 20 93 38 | www.toptours. net)*. The same companies will take you on themed guided walks, such as through the red-light district and the INSIDER TIP *hofjes* in Jordaan. The price per person ranges between 15 and 25 euros, depending on the tour.

Almost every bike-hire operator runs guided tours by bicycle. The most comprehensive programme, including trips out to the IJsselmeer, is on offer at Orange Bike (120 A3) (*ጠ F3*) *(Singel 233 | tel. 020 5 28 99 90 | www.orangebike. nl | tram 1, 2, 5, 13, 17 Dam)* and *Yellow Bike* (120 B2) (*ጠ G3*) *(Nieuwezijds Kolk 29 | tel. 020 6 20 69 40 | www.yellowbike. nl | tram 1, 2, 5, 13, 17 Kolk)*. Prices are around 20 euros for 3 hours including the charge for bike hire.

Bus tours of Amsterdam can also be booked, for example the *Tourist Bus* (120 C2) (*ጠ G3*) *(price 13 euros | duration 1 hour 45 minutes, departures every 30 minutes between 9.30am and 5pm | Damrak 34 | www.touristbusamsterdam. com | 5 min. on foot from the main station)*. Bear in mind, however, that the streets of the old quarter are narrow, and buses can only go along the main roads. If you are looking for an eco-friendly way to get round Amsterdam without walking or pedalling yourself, consider taking a tour on a *Segway* electro-scooter *(tel. 088 0 12 30 50 | www.seg waybooking.com)*. With prices starting at 40 euros for 90 minutes including instruction in how to operate them, they are by no means cheap, but it's a load of fun.

HEALTH

If you need medical aid, contact a general practitioner *(huisarts)*. The huisarts emergency service is available 24 hours a day: *tel. 088 0 03 06 00*. In the Netherlands the European Health Insurance Card (EHIC) is accepted. Private medical insurance is still advisable, and is essential for visitors from outside the European Union.

I AMSTERDAM CITY CARD

The *I amsterdam City Card* for leisure and cultural activities is valid for one, two or three days. It gives you a canal trip at a reduced price or even free of charge, use of public transport and free admission to several museums, e.g. the Van Gogh, Amsterdam and Rijksmuseum. There are also discounts on some other attractions and at restaurants. The pass costs 42 euros (1 day), 52 euros (2 days) or 62 euros (3 days). It is sold at offices of the VVV and online at *www.iamsterdamcard.nl*.

INFORMATION IN ADVANCE

DUTCH BOARD OF TOURISM IN LONDON

PO Box 30 783 | London WC2B 6DH | tel. 020 75 39 79 50 | www.iamsterdam.com and www.holland.com/uk

DUTCH BOARD OF TOURISM IN NEW YORK

355 Lexington Avenue, New York, NY 10017 C212/370-7360; http://us.holland.com

INFORMATION IN AMSTERDAM

AMSTERDAM TOURIST OFFICE (VVV)

The tourist offices offer information and tickets for city tours. The VVV will also find you a hotel or B & B, for a fee. In the peak season expect to stand in a long queue at the office on Stationsplein!

– *Stationsplein 10 (opposite the main station) | Mon–Sat 9am–6pm, Sun 9am–5pm –Schiphol Airport (arrivals hall) | daily 7am–10pm | tel. 020 2 0188 00 | www.vvv.nl*

INTERNET & WIFI

Internet cafés are almost non-existent in Amsterdam, but various cafés and restaurants offer free internet access. *www.wifi-amsterdam.nl* has a citymap showing these places. Free WiFi is provided by the *city library (p. 35)* and in the area around the *Stadtwaage (p. 37)* on the Nieuwmarkt. However, most of the hotels charge a fee of 20 euros for the use of the internet.

MONEY & PRICES

The currency in the Netherlands is the euro. At a supermarket checkout don't be surprised if you get only 50 cents change when it should be 52 cents: in the Netherlands everything is rounded

BUDGETING

Coffee	2.50 euros
	in a koffiehuis for a cup of koffie verkeerd
Beer	2 euros
	for a glass of beer (0.3 litres)
Cinema	10 euros
	for a ticket
Tulips	5 euros
	for 10
Lunch	10 euros
	for a basic lunch
Tram	2.80 euros
	for a tram ticket

to 5 cents. 1 and 2 cent coins are rare. Payment by card is common, even for small amounts. In most restaurants, shops and supermarkets you can pay with a debit card (with the Maestro symbol) and PIN code. Many cafés and small restaurants don't accept credit cards. If you want to pay with a credit card, you must know the PIN code.

OPENING HOURS

From Monday to Friday most shops are open 9am–6pm. On Thursdays city-centre shops stay open until 9pm. On Saturdays you can shop until 6pm, and on Sundays in the city centre from noon till 5pm. Supermarkets open Mon–Sat until 8pm, in the city centre until 10pm, on Sundays till 8pm. Market stalls are in business until about 4pm.

PARKING

There is no free parking within the A10 motorway ring. Parking tickets are bought from machines on the street. In the Centrum, Noord and Oud-West districts you can only pay by debit or credit card, not in cash. In other districts you need coins. The modern machines register your number plate so you don't need to put a ticket behind the windscreen. Costs in the city centre: *5 euros per hr*, day ticket *45 euros (9am–midnight)*. Parking is cheaper outside the centre. The fine for not getting a ticket is 51.90 euros. The fee if you get towed away is approx. 150 euros.

Car parks in Amsterdam city centre *(approx. 40 euros/day): Europarking (Marnixstraat 250); Bijenkorf* department store, *Muziektheater (Waterlooplein), Nieuwezijds Kolk* and *Byzantium (Tesselschadestraat 1)*. Park & ride at the *Transferium Arena (8 euros incl. 5 metro tickets, has to be activated at the cash desk!).* Further information: *www. parkerenindestad.n*

PHONE & MOBILE PHONE

For the green telephone kiosks, which are becoming thin on the ground, you need a phone card, obtainable from a newsagent, post office or the tourist office (VVV).
Codes: UK *0044*, USA *001*, Netherlands *0031*, Amsterdam *(0)20*

POST

Most post offices open Mon–Fri 9am–5pm, Sat 9am–1pm. However, there are fewer of them than there used to be. Stamps are on sale in the *Bruna* chain of newsagents and at the checkouts in the *Albert Heijn* supermarkets. It costs 90 cents to send a postcard or a standard-sized letter to other countries in the EU, 1.05 euros to the US. *www. post.nl*

PUBLIC TRANSPORT

Public transport in Amsterdam consists of trams, buses and a few metro lines. The tickets are electronic cards, which cost 2.80 euros for 1 hour and are valid for the whole of Amsterdam. It is cheaper to buy a day ticket or one for several days. Day tickets are valid for 24 hours, cost 7.50 euros and are sold by the conductor. Tickets for several days are sold only at *GVB Ticket & Info* in front of the main station, from machines at metro stops and at some hotel reception desks.
Trams are entered by the back door, where the conductor sits. The rule for all electronic tickets is that you have to check in when you board and check out again when you leave the tram, even if you are only changing lines! To do this, hold the ticket in front of the reader by the conductor's cabin or at the door until the reader beeps. If you forget to check out, the ticket loses its validity. Amsterdam-Noord is served by buses and free ferries, which all dock on the north side of the main station. Only the ferry to Buiksloterweg runs all night. The others operate until about midnight. On weekdays buses and trams run until around midnight, and at weekends until about 1am. After that there are night buses, with special fares. A single ticket costs 4 euros and is valid for 1.5 hours. *www.gvb.nl*

TAXIS

There are cab ranks at the main station, in front of big hotels and on major squares such as Leidseplein. It's rather difficult to hail taxis on the street, as many simply don't stop. Even if the drivers will tell you a different story: you are free to choose which taxi you take! *Tel. 020 6 77 77 77 | www.tcataxi.nl | flat rate for the first 2 km 7.50 euros, after that 1.95 euros per km.*
Between the railway station and the Victoria Hotel there is a special rank for ☺ green taxis. This catagory includes Motor Cabs with electric drive as well as the so called *Clean Cabs* that look a little bit like a golf caddy. The centre of Amsterdam is also served by bicycle rickshaws. You can stop one on the street or order one under *tel. 06 28 24 75 50*. They also have bases on the Dam and Leidseplein. The trip costs 5 euros per passenger per 10 minutes. *www.wielertaxi.nl*

TIPPING

In taxis, restaurants and cafés you round up the amount to be paid to make a tip of five to ten per cent. For room service in a hotel 1–2 euros per day.

USEFUL PHRASES DUTCH

PRONUNCIATION

To help you with the pronunciation we have added to each word or phrase a simplified guide on how to say it [in square brackets]. Here kh denotes a guttural sound similar to 'ch' in Scottish 'loch', and ü is spoken like 'u' in French 'tu'.

IN BRIEF

Yes/No/Maybe	ja [ya]/nee [nay]/misschien [miss-kheen]
Please/	alstublieft [ashtübleeft]/alsjeblieft
Thank you	[ash-yer-bleeft]/bedankt [bedankt]
Excuse me	Sorry [sorry]
May I ...?/ Pardon?	Mag ik ...? [makh ick]/ Pardon? [*spoken as in French*]
I would like to .../	Ik wil graag ... [ick vill khraakh]/
Have you got ...?	Heeft u ...? [hayft ü]
How much is ...	Hoeveel kost ...? [hoofayl kost]
I (don't) like that	Dat vind ik (niet) leuk. [dat find ick (niet) lurk]
broken/doesn't work	kapot [kapott]/werkt niet [vairkt neet]
Help!/Attention!/	Hulp! [hülp]/Let op! [lett opp]/
Caution!	Voorzichtig!/[forzikhtikh]
Ambulance	ambulance [ambülantser]
Police/Fire brigade	politie [politsee]/brandweer [brandvayr]

GREETINGS, FAREWELL

Good morning!/afternoon!/	Goeden morgen/dag! [khooyer morkhe/dakh]/
evening!/night!	avond!/nacht! [afond/nakht]
Hello!/goodbye!	Hallo! [hallo]/Dag! [daakh]
See you	Doei! [dooee]
My name is ...	Ik heet ... [ick hayt]
What's your name?	Hoe heet u? [hoo hayt ü]/Hoe heet je? [hoo hayt yer]
I'm from ...	Ik kom uit ... [ick komm owt]

DATE AND TIME

Monday/Tuesday	maandag [maandakh]/dinsdag [dinnsdakh]
Wednesday/Thursday	woensdag [voonsdakh]/donderdag [donderdakh]
Friday/Saturday	vrijdach [fraydakh]/zaterdag [zatterdakh]
Sunday/holiday	zondag [zonndakh]/feestdag [faystdakh]

Spreek jij nederlands?

"Do you speak Dutch?" This guide will help you to say the basic words and phrases in Dutch.

today/tomorrow/ yesterday	vandaag [fanndaakh]/morgen (morkher]/ gisteren (khisteren]
What time is it?	Hoe laat is het? [hoo laat iss hett]
It's three o'clock	Het is drie uur [hett iss dree üür]

TRAVEL

open/closed	open [open]/gesloten [khesloten]
entrance	ingang [innkhang]/inrit [inritt]
exit	uitgang [owtkhang]/*(car park)* uitrit [owtritt], *(motorway)* afslag [affslakh]
departure/ arrival	vertrektijd [fertrekktayt]/vertrek [fertrekk]/ aankomst [aankommst]
toilets women/men	toilet [twalett]/dames [daamers]/heren [hayren]
(not) drinking water	(geen) drinkwater [(kheen) drinkvaater]
Where is ...?/Where are ...?	Waar is ...? [vaar iss]/Waar zijn ...? [vaar zayn]
left/right/ straight ahead/ back/close/far	links [links]/rechts [rekhts]/ rechtdoor [rekhtdor]/ terug [terükh]/dichtbij [dikhtbay]/ver [fair]
bus/tram	bus [büs]/tram [tram]
U-underground / taxi/cab	metro [metro] / taxi [taxi]
bus stop/cab stand	station [stasseeonn]/taxistandplaats [taxistandplaats]
parking lot/ parking garage	parkplaats [parkplaats]/ parkeergarage [parkayrkharager]
train station/harbour	station [stasseeonn]/haven [haafen]
airport	luchthaven [lükhthaafen]
timetable/ticket	dienstregeling [dienstraykheling]/kaartje [kaartyer]
single/return	enkel [enkel]/retour [retour]
train / track/platform	trein [trayn] / spoor [spoor]/perron [peronn]
I would like to rent ...	Ik wil graag ... huren [ick vill khraakh ... hüüren]
a car/a bicycle/a boat	een auto [enn owto]/fiets [feets]/boot [boat]
petrol / gas station	tankstation [tankstasseeonn]
petrol/gas / diesel	benzine [benseen]/diesel [diesel]

FOOD & DRINK

Could you please book a table for tonight for four?	Wilt u alstublieft voor vanavond een tafel voor vier personen voor ons reserveren. [villt ü ashtübleeft for fannaafont en taafel for feer pairzonen for ons reservayren]
on the terrace/ by the window	op het terras [opp het terrass]/ bij het raam [bay het raam]
The menu, please	De kaart, alstublieft. [de kaart ashtübleeft]

Could I please have ...?	Mag ik ...? [makh ick]
bottle/carafe/glass	fles [fless]/karaf [karaff]/glas [khlass]
a knife/a fork/a spoon	mes [mess]/fork [fork]/lepel [laypel]
salt/pepper/sugar	zout [zowt]/peper [payper]/suiker [zowker]
vinegar/oil	azijn [azayn]/olie [olee]
with/without ice/sparkling	met [mett]/zonder ijs [zonder ays]/bubbels [bübbels]
May I have the bill, please?	Mag ik afrekenen [makh ick affraykenen]
bill/receipt	rekening [raykening]/bonnetje [bonnetyer]

SHOPPING

Where can I find...?	Waar vind ik...? [vaar finnt ick]
I'd like .../I'm looking for ...	Ik wil ... [ick vill]/Ik zoek ... [ick zook]
pharmacy/chemist	apotheek [apotayk]/drogisterij [drookhisteray]
department store	winkelcentrum [vinkelzentrümm]
supermarket	supermarkt [züpermarkt]
100 grammes/1 kilo	1 ons [onz]/1 kilo [kilo]
expensive/cheap/price	duur [düür]/goedkoop [khootkoap]/prijs [prayss]
more/less	meer [mayr]/minder [minder]

ACCOMMODATION

I have booked a single/ double room	Ik heb een eenpersoonskamer/tweepersoonskamer gereserveerd [ick hepp en aynperzoanskaamer/ tvayperzoanskaamer khereservayrt]
Do you have any ... left?	Heeft u nog ... [hayft ü nokh]
breakfast/half board	ontbijt [ontbayt]/halfpension [hallfpenseeonn]
full board (American plan)	volpension [follpenseeonn]
at the front/seafront	naar de voorkant/zee [naar de forkannt/zay]
shower/sit-down bath	douche [doosh]/badkamer [battkaamer]
balcony/terrace	balkon [balkonn]/terras [terrass]
key/room card	sleutel [slurtel]/sleutelkaart [slurtelkaart]

BANKS, MONEY & CREDIT CARDS

| bank/ATM | bank [bank]/pinautomat [pinn-owtomaat] |
| cash/credit card | kontant [kontant]/pinpas [pinnpass]/ creditcard [kreditkaart] |

HEALTH

doctor/dentist/ paediatrician	arts [arts]/tandarts [tandarts]/ kinderarts [kinderarts]
hospital/ emergency clinic	ziekenhuis [zeekenhows]/ spoedeisende hulp[spootayzender hülp]
fever/pain	koorts [koorts]/pijn [payn]

diarrhoea/nausea	diaree [diaray]/misselijkheid [misselick-hayt]
inflamed/injured	ontstoken [ontstoaken]/gewond [khevonnt]
pain reliever/tablet	pijnstiller [paynstiller]/tablet [tablett]

POST, TELECOMMUNICATIONS & MEDIA

stamp/letter/ postcard	zegel [zaykhel]/brief [breef]/ aanzichtkaart [aanzikhtkaart]
I need a landline phone card	Ik wil graag een telefoonkaart voor het vaste net. [ick vill khraakh en telephonekaart for het faster net]
I need a prepaid card for my mobile	Ik zoek een prepaid-kaart voor mijn mobieltje. [ick zook en prepaid-kaart for mayn mobeelt-yer]
Where can I find internet access?	Waar krijg ik toegang tot internet [vaar kraykh ick too-khang tot internet]
socket/adapter/ charger	stopcontact [stoppkontakt]/adapter [adapter]/ oplader [oplaader]
computer/battery/ rechargeable battery	computer [computer]/batterij [batteray]/ accu [akkü]
internet connection/wifi	internetverbinding [internetferbinnding]/WLAN
e-mail/file/ print	mail [mail]/bestand [bestant]/ uitdraaien [owtdraa-yen]

LEISURE, SPORTS & BEACH

beach/bathing beach	strand [strand]/strandbad [strandbart]
sunshade/ lounger	zonnescherm [zonner sherm]/ zonnestoel [zonnerstool]
low tide/high tide	laagwater [laakhvaater]/hoogwater [hoakhvaater]

NUMBERS

0	nul [nüll]	15	vijftien [fayfteen]
1	één [ayn]	16	zestien [zesteen]
2	twee [tvay]	17	zeventien [zerventeen]
3	drie [dree]	18	achtien [akhteen]
4	vier [feer]	19	negentien [naykhenteen]
5	vijf [fayf]	70	zeventig [zerventikh]
6	zes [zess]	80	tachtig [takhtikh]
7	zeven [zerven]	90	negentig [naykhentikh]
8	acht [akht]	100	honderd [hondert]
9	negen [naykhen]	200	tweehonderd [tvayhondert]
10	tien [teen]	1000	duizend [dowzent]
11	elf [elf]	2000	tweeduizend [tvaydowzent]
12	twaalf [tvaalf]	10000	tienduizend [teendowzent]
13	dertien [dairteen]	1/2	half [hallf]
14	viertien [feerteen]	1/4	kwart [kvart]

NOTES

MARCO POLO TRAVEL GUIDES

ALGARVE
AMSTERDAM
ANDALUCÍA
ATHENS
AUSTRALIA
AUSTRIA
BALI
  LOMBOK,
  GILI ISLANDS
BANGKOK
BARCELONA
BERLIN
BRAZIL
BRUGES, GHENT &
  ANTWERP
BRUSSELS
BUDAPEST
BULGARIA
CALIFORNIA
CAMBODIA
CANADA EAST
CANADA WEST
  ROCKIES
CAPE TOWN
  WINE LANDS, GAR-
  DEN ROUTE
CAPE VERDE
CHANNEL ISLANDS
CHICAGO
  & THE LAKES
CHINA
COLOGNE
COPENHAGEN
CORFU
COSTA BLANCA
  VALENCIA
COSTA BRAVA
  BARCELONA
COSTA DEL SOL
  GRANADA
CRETE
CUBA
CYPRUS
  NORTH AND
  SOUTH
DRESDEN
DUBAI
DUBLIN
DUBROVNIK & DALMA-
  TIAN COAST

EDINBURGH
EGYPT
EGYPT'S RED SEA RE-
  SORTS
FINLAND
FLORENCE
FLORIDA
FRENCH ATLANTIC
  COAST
FRENCH RIVIERA
  NICE, CANNES & MO-
  NACO
FUERTEVENTURA
GRAN CANARIA
GREECE
HAMBURG
HONG KONG
  MACAU
ICELAND
INDIA
INDIA SOUTH
  GOA & KERALA
IRELAND
ISRAEL
ISTANBUL
ITALY
JORDAN
KOS
KRAKOW
LAKE GARDA

LANZAROTE
LAS VEGAS
LISBON
LONDON
LOS ANGELES
MADEIRA
  PORTO SANTO
MADRID
MALLORCA
MALTA
  GOZO
MAURITIUS
MENORCA
MILAN
MONTENEGRO
MOROCCO
MUNICH
NAPLES &
  THE AMALFI COAST
NEW YORK
NEW ZEALAND
NORWAY
OSLO
PARIS
PHUKET
PORTUGAL
PRAGUE

RHODES
ROME
SAN FRANCISCO
SARDINIA
SCOTLAND
SEYCHELLES
SHANGHAI
SICILY
SINGAPORE
SOUTH AFRICA
SRI LANKA
STOCKHOLM
SWITZERLAND
TENERIFE
THAILAND
TURKEY
TURKEY
  SOUTH COAST
TUSCANY
UNITED ARAB EMIRA-
  TES
USA SOUTHWEST
VENICE
VIENNA
VIETNAM
ZÁKYNTHOS

MARCO POLO
With Road Atlas & Pull-Out Map
FRENCH RIVIERA
NICE, CANNES & MONACO
SPECTACULAR GRAND CANYON DU VERDON
Breath-taking scenery that takes some beating
SNIFFING THE AIR
The perfume manufacturers of Grasse
Travel with Insider Tips
www.marco-polo.com

MARCO POLO
EW YORK
RS, WILD FLOWERS AND SKYSCRAPERS
The High Line in Chelsea
ON CLOUD NINE
Stay at 230 Fifth Street
Travel with Insider Tips

MARCO POLO
ROAD ATLAS & PULL-OUT MAP
KE GARDA
BALDO WITH MOUNTAIN BIKE
the Malcesine takes bikes too
SES" IN SALÒ
late "Kaonly"
Travel with Insider Tips

MARCO POLO
With Street Atlas & Pull-Out Map
BERLIN
A STUNNING ISLAND JUST FOR ART
Showcasing treasures from around the world
COOL AT NIGHT
rlin club scene sets the trend
Travel with Insider Tips

MARCO POLO
With Road Atlas & Pull-Out Map
ALLORCA
W FLAIR IN THE MEDITERRANEAN
llorca's most beautiful beach
IN" CROWD MEET
za in Deià
Travel with Insider Tips

- PACKED WITH INSIDER TIPS
- BEST WALKS AND TOURS
- FULL-COLOUR PULL-OUT MAP
  AND STREET ATLAS

STREET ATLAS

The green line ████ **indicates the Walking tours (p. 94–99)**

All tours are also marked on the pull-out map

Photo: Pedalling across Prinsengracht

Exploring Amsterdam

The map on the back cover shows how the area has been sub-divided

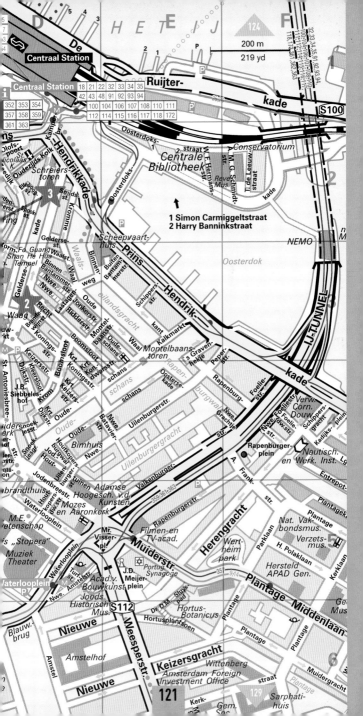

Map labels

D · **H E T I J** · **E** · **I J** · **F**

124

200 m
219 yd

De
Centraal Station

Centraal Station
18 · 21 · 22 · 32 · 33 · 34 · 35
42 · 43 · 48 · 91 · 92 · 93 · 94
100 · 104 · 106 · 107 · 108 · 110 · 111
112 · 114 · 115 · 116 · 117 · 118 · 172

352 · 353 · 354
357 · 358 · 359
361 · 363

Ruijter-
kade

S100

Oosterdoks-
1
Oosterdoks-
2 straat
W. F. Hermans-straat
Conservatorium
A. M. G. Schmidt-straat
I. de Leeuw-kade
Reve-Mus.

Centrale
Bibliotheek

1 Simon Carmiggeltstraat
2 Harry Banninkstraat

NEMO

Oosterdok

Olofs-
poort
Nicolaas
Oudezijds Kolk
Schreiers-
toren
Smidt-
st.
Kromme
Waal

Gelderse-
st.
Gelderse-
kade
Nwe.
Recht
Boomssloot

Scheepvaart-
huis
Prins
Buiten
Bantammerstr.
Schippers-
str.
kant
Kalkmarkt
s Graven-
hekje
Peper-
str.
Rapenburg-
str.
Foelie-
str.
Verw.
Corn.
Douw
Schippers-
gracht
Kadijks-
plein

Prins Hendrik-
kade

IJ-TUNNEL

kade

Waag-
kt

Binnen
Bantammer
Binnen
Waal
Oude
Waal
Moptelbaans-
toren
Oosterse-
kade
Rapenburg-
Rapenburg
Foelie-
dw.str.
Nwe. Foeliestr.

St. Antonies-
bree-

J.B.
Siebbeleshof
Konings-
st.
Keizers-
st.
Krom
Oude-
Oude-
Boomssloot
Koningssstr.
Kr.
Kon.
Keizers-
Kr.
Keizers-
Dijkstr.
Montel-
baanstr.
Oude-
schans
Waal
Tapen-
burgwal
schans
Nwe.
Batavier-
str.
Uilenburgerstr.
Uilenburgergracht
Nwe.
A. Frank-
str.
Rapenburger-
plein
Nautisch
en Werk. Inst.
Entrepot-

iderssnoek-
kerk-
hof
lem-
jestr.
oten-
Bimhuis
Jod.
Houtk.
burgwal
Uilen-
Houtk.
Hout.
Uilenburgergracht
Oude-
schans

brandthuise
Waterlooplein
Jodenbreestr. Hoogesch. v.d.
Hoogesch.
Adamse
Kunsten
Mozes
en Aäronkerk
Valkenburger-
Valkenburgerstr.
Rapenburgerstr.

Plantage
Nat. Vak-
bondsmus.
Plantage
Verzets-
mus.
H. Polaklaan
Ketklaan
Plantagekade

M.E.
Wetenschap
's "Stopera"
Muziek
Theater
Waterlooplein

Mr.
Visser-
pl.
Filmen-en
TV-acad.
Muiderstr.
Herengracht
Wert-
heim
park
Hersteld
APAD Gen.
Ge.
Mus

Acad.v.
Bouwkunst
Joods
Historisch Mus.
Turfst.
Amstelstr.
J.D.
Meijer-
plein
Portug.
Synagoge
De D.M. Sluys
pad
Hortus-
Botanicus
Hortusplantsoen
Plantage Middenlaan
Plantage

Blauw.
brug
Amstel
Amstelhof
Nieuwe
Nwe.
Weesperstr.
S112
Keizersgracht
Wittenberg
Amsterdam Foreign
Investment Office
Gem.
Soc.
Kerk-
straat
Muidergracht
Plantage
Sarphati-
huis

Nieuwe

121

129

S. Antoniesbree-
Fo Guang
Shan He Hua
Tempel
Waals-
str.
Binnenkant
Ridderstr.
Jonkerstr.
eilandsgracht

Schreierstoren
Montelbaanstr.

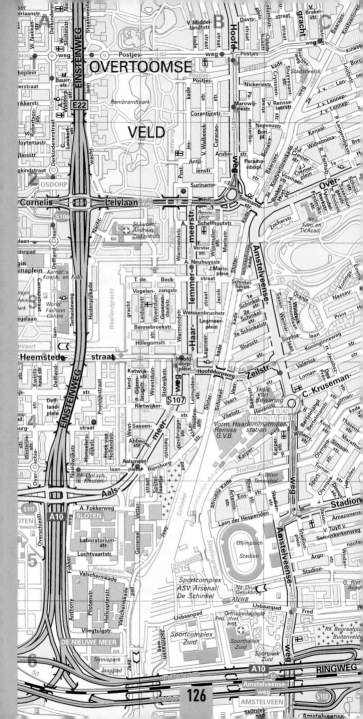

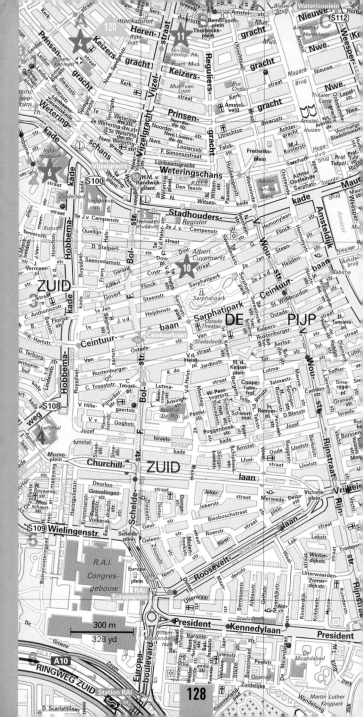

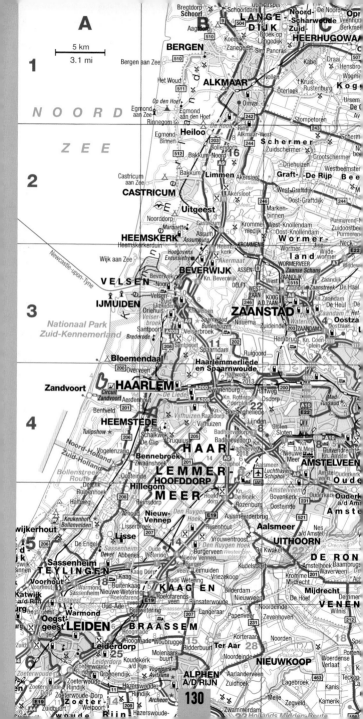

This index contains a selection of the streets and squares shown on the street atlas

A

A. Durerstraat 127/E4
Aalsmeerplein 126/A4-B4
Aalsmeerweg 126/A5-B4
Achillesstraat 126/C5-127/D5
Achtergracht 128/C2
Adama van Scheltemaplein 127/E4
Adelaarsweg 124/B2-C1
Admiraal de Ruijterweg 122/A2-B5
Admiralengracht 122/A4-A6
Afrikanerplein 129/D3-E3
Agamemnonstraat 126/C5
Agnietenstraat, Sint 120/C4
Albasstraat 128/B5-B6
Albert Cuypstraat 128/A3-B2
Alexanderplein 129/E1
Amstel 120/B5-121/D6
Amsteldijk 128/C2-129/D5
Amstelkade 128/B4-129/D4
Amstelstraat 120/C6
Amstelveenseweg 126/B2-C6
Amstelveld 128/B1
Anna v. d. Vondelstraat 127/D2
Anne Frankstraat 121/F4-F5
Annendwarsstraat, Sint 120/C3
Annenstraat, Sint 120/C3
Anthony Fokkerweg 126/A5-A6
Antillenstraat 126/B2
Antoniesbreestraat, Sint 121/D4
Apollolaan 127/D4-F4
Argonautenstraat 126/C5
Asterweg 124/A1-A2

B

Baarsstraat 126/B4
Badhuisweg 124/A2
Baerlestraat, van 127/E2-F3
Bakkersstraat 120/C5-C6
Balboastraat 122/A5
Balistraat 129/F1
Balk in 't Oogstraat 120/C5-C6
Banckersweg Joos 122/A4
Bankastraat 129/F1
Banstraat 127/E3
Barberenstraat, Sint 120/B4
Barentszplein 123/E1
Barentszstraat 123/E1
Barndesteeg 120/C3
Baroniestraat 128/B6
Baststraat Pieter 128/A3
Beethovenstraat 127/E4-E6
Beetsstraat Nicolaas 127/D1
Begijnensteeg 120/B4
Begijnhof 120/A4
Beijersweg 129/F2-F3
Bellamyplein 122/B5-C6
Bellamystraat 122/B6
Bentinckstraat 122/C2
Berenstraat 123/D5
Bergstraat 120/A2
Bernard Kochstraat 126/C4
Bernard Zweerskade 127/E5-F4
Bertelmanstraat 126/C4
Bestevaerstraat 122/B2-B3
Bethaniëndwarsstraat 120/C4
Bethaniënstraat 120/C4
Beulingstraat 120/A5
Beuningenplein, van 122/C3
Beuningenstraat, van 122/C3-123/D2
Beursplein 120/C3
Beursstraat 120/C2
Bickersgracht 123/E2
Bickersstraat 123/E2

Biesboschstraat 128/B5
Bilderdijkkade 122/C5-C6
Bilderdijkstraat 122/C5-C6
Binnen Bantammerstraat 121/D3
Binnen Vissersstraat 123/E3-F3
Binnen Wieringerstraat 123/E3
Binnengasthuisstraat 120/B5
Binnenkant 121/D2-E3
Blasiusstraat 128/C3-129/D2
Blauwbrug 121/D6
Blauwburgwal 120/A2-B2
Blindemansteeg 120/B6
Bloedstraat 120/C3-121/D3
Bloemenmarkt 120/A5-B6
Bloemgracht 123/D4
Boerensteeg 120/C4
Bonairestraat 126/B1-B2
Boomsteeg 121/D3
Boorstraat 120/B6
Borgerstraat 126/C1-127/D1
Borneokade 125/E5-F5
Borneostraat 125/D6-E6
Borssenburgplein 128/C4
Bos en Lommerweg 122/A2-A3
Bossestraat, van 122/C3
Brandewijnsteeg 121/D3
Brandts Buysstr. 127/D5
Breestraat, van 127/D3-E2
Brielstraat, den 122/A2-B3
Brouwersgracht 120/B1-YY/A3
Buijskade 122/C4
Buiksloterweg 124/A3-C1
Buiten Bantammerstraat 121/E3
Buiten Brouwersstraat 123/D2-E3
Buiten Vissersstraat 123/E3-F3
Buiten Wieringerstraat 123/E3
Burmanstraat 129/D3

C

C. van Eesterenlaan 125/E5
Cabotstraat 122/A5
Camperstraat 129/D2
Ceintuurbaan 128/A3-C3
Celebesstraat 129/F1-F2
Cellebroerssteeg 120/B4
Chassestraat 122/B5-B6
Chrysantenstraat 124/A1
Churchillaan 128/B4-C4
Clerqstraat de 122/B5-C5
Columbusplein 126/B1-C1
Commelinstraat 129/E1-F1
Concertgebouwplein 127/E3
Constantijn Huygensstraat, 1e 122/C6-127/E2
Contactweg 122/A1
Cooperatiehof 128/C4
Corantijnstraat 126/B1-B2
Cornelis Krusemanstraat 126/C4-127/D3
Cornelis Schuytstraat 127/D3-E3
Cremerplein J. J. 126/C2
Cruquiuskade 124/C6-125/D6
Cruquiusweg 125/D5-F5
Crynssenstraat 126/C1-C2
Curaçaostraat 126/B1-B2
Czaar Peterstraat 124/C6-D5

D

Da Costakade 122/C5-C6
Da Costaplein 122/C5
Da Costastraat 122/C5-C6
Dam 120/B3
Damrak 120/B3-C2
Damraksteeg 120/B3

Damstraat 120/B3-C3
De Lairessestraat 127/D3-E3
De Mirandalaan 128/C6
Delflandlaan 126/A2-A4
Deltastraat 128/C5
Derkinderenstraat 126/A1-A2
Des Présstraat 126/C4
Deurloostraat 128/A5-B5
Diemenstraat, van 123/E1
Diepenbrockstraat 127/E4-F5
Dijk Keizerstraat 121/D3-D4
Dijksgracht 124/B4-C4
Dijkstraat 121/D4
Dintelstraat 128/B5-B6
Distelweg 124/A1-B1
Domselaerstraat 129/F2
Dr. D. M. Sluyspad 121/E5-E6
Driekoningenstraat 120/A3
Droogbak 123/F3
Dubbeleworststeeg 120/A5
Duifjessteeg 120/B4
Duivendrechtsekade 129/F6

E

E. Wolffstraat 122/B5-C5
Edammerstraat 125/F1
Eeghenstraat, van 127/D3-E2
Eemsstraat 125/D6-D5
Egelantiersgracht 123/D4
Eggerstraat 120/B3
Egidiusstraat 122/A3-A4
Eikenplein 129/E2
Elandsgracht 123/E5
Elandsstraat 123/D5
Elleboogsteeg 121/D2
Emmastraat 127/D3
Enge Kapelsteeg 120/B4
Enge Kerksteeg 120/C2
Enge Lombardsteeg 120/B4
Entrepotbrug 125/E5
Entrepotdok 124/B5-B6
Europaplein 128/A5-B5

F

Fagelstraat 122/C3-123/D3
Fahrenheitsingel 129/E5
Fahrenheitstraat 129/E5-F5
Fannius Scholtenstraat 122/C2-C3
Ferdinand Bolstraat 128/A2-A4
Fizeaustraat 129/E5-F5
Flevoweg 125/F6
Foeliedwarsstraat 121/F4
Foeliestraat 121/F4
Frans Halsstraat 128/A2-A3
Frans van Mierisstraat 127/E3-F3
Fred Roeskestraat 126/C6-ZZ/D6
Frederik Hendrikplantsoen 122/C3-123/D3
Frederik Hendrikstraat 122/C3-C5

G

Gabriël Metsustraat 127/E3-F3
Gapersteeg 120/B4
Gasthuismolenstraat 120/A3
Gebed Zonder End 120/B4
Gedempte 124/B2-B3
Geelvinckssteeg 120/B6
Geertruidensteeg, Sint 120/B2
Geldersekade 121/D2-D3
Geldersesteeg 121 D2-D3
Geleenstraat 128/B5
Gen. Vetterstraat 126/A5-B5
Gerard Doustraat 128/A3-B2
Gerrit v. d. Veenstraat 127/D4-E4
Geulstraat 128/B5

Geuzenkade **122/B4-B5**
Geuzenstraat **122/B4-B5**
Gevleweg **123/D1**
Gillis van Ledenberchstraat **122/C4**
Gooiseweg **129/E4-F5**
Gorontalostraat **125/E6**
Gouwenaarsteeg **120/B1**
Govert Flinckstraat **128/A3-C2**
Graswegg **124/A1-A2**
Gravelandse Veer, 's- **120/C5**
Gravenhekje, 's- **121/E3**
Gravenstraat **120/B3**
Gravesandeplein, 's- **129/D2**
Gravesandestraat, 's- **129/D1-D2**
Grimburgwal **120/B4**
Groen van Prinstererstraat **122/C2-C3**
Groenburgwal **120/C4-C5**
Grote Wittenburgerstraat **124/C5**
Guerickestraat, Von **129/E5-F5**

H
H. Ronnerplein **128/C4**
H.A.J Baanderskade **125/E6-F6**
Haarlemmerdijk **123/D1-E3**
Haarlemmer-Houttuinen **123/E2-F3**
Haarlemmermeerstraat **126/B2-B3**
Haarlemmerplein **123/D2**
Haarlemmerstraat **123/E3-F3**
Haarlemmerweg **122/A2**
Hagedoornweg **124/B1**
Hallstraat, van **122/C2-C3**
Halvemaansteeg **120/C5-C6**
Hamerkade **124/C2**
Hamerstraat **124/C2**
Handboogstraat **120/A5**
Handelskade **125/D4-E4**
Haringpakkerssteeg **120/C2**
Hartenstraat **123/E5**
Hasebroekstraat **122/B6**
Hasselaerssteeg **120/C1**
Hasseltssteeg, D. van **120/B2**
Havenstraat **126/B4-C4**
Havikslaan **124/A2**
Hectorstraat **127/D5**
Heemstedestraat **126/A3-B3**
Heiligeweg **120/A5-B5**
Heimansweg **124/A1-B2**
Heintje Hoekssteeg **120/C2**
Heisteeg **120/A5**
Hekelveld **120/B1-C1**
Helmersstraat, 1e **126/C2-127/E1**
Helststraat, 1e van der **128/B3**
Helststraat, 2e van der **128/B3-B4**
Hembrugstraat **122/C1-123/D1**
Hemonylaan **128/B2-C2**
Hendrik Jacobszstraat **126/C3-C4**
Henri Polaklaan **121/F5**
Henrick de Keijserstraat **128/B3**
Herculesstraat **126/C4-C5**
Herengracht **120/B1-121/D6**
Herenmarkt **123/E3**
Herenstraat **120/A1-A2**
Herman Heijermansweg **128/A4-A5**
Hermietenstraat **120/B3**
Hertspiegelweg **122/A3**
Hilligaertstraat, van **128/A4**
Hobbemakade **127/F2-F4**
Hobbemastraat **127/F2**
Hodenpijlkade **126/A3**
Hoekschewaardweg **125/D1**
Hogendorpstraat, van **122/B3-123/D2**
Holbeinstraat **127/E5**

Hondecoeterstraat **127/E3**
Honthorststraat **127/E2-F2**
Hoofddorpplein **126/B3-B4**
Hoofddorpweg **126/B4**
Hoofdweg **122/A5-126/B2**
Hoogte Kadijk **124/B5-C6**
Hoopstraat, van der **122/C2**
Hortusplantsoen **121/E6**
Houtkopersburgwal **121/D4**
Houtkopersdwarsstraat **121/D5**
Houtmankade **123/D2-E1**
Hudsonstraat **122/A5-A6**
Hugo de Grootplein **122/C4**
Hugo de Grootstraat, 1e **122/C4**
Hugo de Grootstraat, 2e **122/C4**
Hugo de Vrieslaan **129/E5-F4**
Huidekoperstraat **128/B2**
Huidenstraat **123/E5**
Hunzestraat **128/C5-C6**
Hygiëaplein **126/C4-127/D4**

I
Ijsbaanpad **126/B6-C6**
Ijselstraat **128/B4-C4**
IJ-Tunnel **124/C1-B5**

J
J. F. van Hengelstraat **125/E4-F4**
J. J. Viottastraat **127/D3-E3**
Jacob Catskade **122/C3**
Jacob Marisplein **126/B3**
Jacob Marisstraat **126/B2-B3**
Jacob Obrechtstraat **127/E2-E3**
Jacob van Lennepkade **126/C1-127/D1**
Jacob van Lennepstraat **126/C1-127/E1**
Jacobsdwarsstraat, Sint **120/C2**
Jacobsstraat, Sint **120/B2-C2**
James Wattstraat **129/E4-F3**
Jan Evertsenstraat **122/A5-B5**
Jan Luijkenstraat **127/E2-F2**
Jan Pieter Heijestraat **126/C1-127/D2**
Jan Schaefferbrug **124/C3-C4**
Jan Sluijterstraat **126/A2**
Jan van der Heijdenstraat, 1e **128/A3-B3**
Jan van Galenstraat **122/A5-C4**
Jan van Goyenkade **127/D3-D4**
Jan Willem Brouwersstraat **127/E3**
Jansstraat, Sint **120/C3**
Jasonstraat **126/C5**
Javakade **124/C3-125/D4**
Javastraat **129/F1**
Jekerstraat **128/B5**
Jereonsteeg **120/B1**
Jodenbreestraat **121/D4-D5**
Jodenhouttuinen **121/D4-D5**
Joh. M. Coenenstraat **127/E2-F2**
Johan van Hasseltweg **124/B1-125/D2**
Johannes Verhulststraat **127/D3-F3**
Jorisstraat, Sint **120/A5-A6**
Jozef Israëlskade **128/B4-129/D4**
Julianaplein **129/E4-E5**

K
K. Doormanstraat **122/A3-B3**
K.N.S.M.-Laan **125/E4-F4**
Kadijksplein **121/F4**
Kalfsvelsteeg **120/B4**
Kalkmarkt **121/E3**
Kalverstraat **120/B3-B5**
Kamerlingh Onneslaan **129/E4-F3**
Kanaalstraat **126/C2-127/D1**
Karnemelksteeg **120/C2**

Karperweg **126/B4-C4**
Karthuizersstraat **123/D3**
Kastanjeplein **129/E2**
Katestraat, ten **122/B6-C6**
Kattenburgerstraat **124/B5-C4**
Kattengat **120/B2**
Keizerrijk **120/A3**
Keizersgracht **123/E3-128/C1**
Kempenaerstraat, de **122/C3**
Kerkstraat **127/F1-128/C1**
Ketelstraat **124/C3**
Kijkduinstraat **122/A2-A3**
Kinderdijkstraat **128/C5-C6**
Kinkerstraat **122/B6-C5**
Kinsbergenstraat, van **122/A5-B5**
Kleersloot **121/D4**
Klimopweg **120/B1**
Klooster **120/B5**
Kloveniersburgwal **120/C4-C5**
Koestraat **120/C3**
Koggestraat **120/B1**
Kolksteeg **120/B2-C2**
Koninginneweg **126/C3-127/D3**
Koningslaan **126/C3-127/D3**
Koningsplein **120/A5**
Koningsstraat **120/C3**
Korsjespoortstraat **120/B1**
Korte Dijkstraat **121/D4**
Korte Keizerstraat **121/D4**
Korte Kolksteeg **120/B2**
Korte Koningsstraat **121/D4**
Korte Korsjespoortsteeg **120/B2**
Korte Lijnbaansteeg **120/B2**
Korte Niezel **120/C2-121/D2**
Korte Reguliersdwarsstraat **120/B6-C6**
Korte Spinhuissteeg **120/C4**
Korte Stormsteeg **120/C3**
Kostverlorenkade, 2e **122/C3-126/C2**
Kostverlorenkade, 3e **126/C2**
Kreupelsteeg **120/C3**
Krom Boomssloot **121/D3-D4**
Kromme Mijdrechtstraat **128/C5-129/D5**
Kromme Waal **121/D2-D3**
Krugerplein **129/E3**
Kruislaan **129/F5-F6**
Kuinderstraat **128/C5-C6**

L
Lange Niezel **120/C2**
Langebrugsteeg **120/B5**
Langestraat **120/B3**
Lastageweg **121/D3**
Lauriergracht **123/D5**
Lavanthkade **125/E4**
Leeuwarderweg **124/C1**
Legmeerstraat **126/B3**
Leidekkerssteeg **120/C3**
Leidsegracht **123/D6-E6**
Leidseplein **127/F1**
Leidsestraat **123/D6**
Leimuidenstraat **126/B4**
Lekstraat **128/C5**
Leliegracht **123/E4**
Leonardostraat **127/D5**
Liebigweg, Von **129/E6-F5**
Lijnbaansgracht **123/D3-D4**
Lijnbaansssteeg **120/B2**
Lindengracht **123/D3-E3**
Linnaeuskade **129/F3**
Linnaeusparkweg **129/F3**
Linnaeusstraat **129/E1-F3**
Lomanstraat **126/C3-C4**
Looiersgracht **123/D5-D6**

This index contains a selection of the streets and squares shown on the street atlas

Lootsstraat **126/C1**
Luciensteeg Sint **120/A4-B4**
Lutmastraat **128/B4-C3**

M

Maasstraat **128/B4-B6**
Madurastraat **129/F1**
Mandenmakerssteeg **120/C2**
Marathonweg **126/C4-127/D5**
Marco Polostraat **122/A5-A6**
Marnixplein **122/C4-123/D4**
Marnixstraat **123/D3**
Martelaarsgracht **120/C1**
Mauritskade **128/C2-129/F1**
Mauvestraat **128/C4**
Meester Treublaan **129/D4**
Meeuwenlaan **124/A3-C2**
Meidoornweg **124/B2**
Meijerplein, J. D. **121/E5**
Mercatorplein **122/A5**
Merwedeplein **128/B5-C5**
Mesdagstraat **128/B4**
Michelangelostraat **127/D4-D5**
Middenweg **129/F3**
Minervalaan **127/D4-D5**
Minervapad **127/D5-E5**
Minervaplein **127/D4-D5**
Moddermolenstraat **121/D4**
Molensteeg **121/D3**
Molsteeg **120/A3-B3**
Monnikenstraat **120/C3-121/D3**
Monnkendammerplantsoen **125/F1**
Monnkendammerweg **125/F1-F2**
Montelbaanstraat **121/D3-E3**
Mosplein **124/B1**
Mosterdpotsteeg **120/B2**
Mosveld **124/B1**
Mozes en Aäronstraat **120/B3**
Mr. Visserplein **121/D5-E5**
Muiderstraat **121/E5**
Muntplein **120/B5**
Museumplein **127/E3-F2**
Muzenplein **127/F4**

N

Naaldwijkstraat **126/A4-A5**
Nadorst Steeg **120/B3-B4**
Nassaukade **123/D2-D6**
Nes **120/B4**
Neuwendammerstraat **125/E1**
Nicolaas Maesstraat **127/E3-F3**
Nicolaasstraat, Sint **120/B2**
Niersstraat **128/B5**
Nieuw Markt **121/D3**
Nieuwe Achtergracht **128/C1-129/D1**
Nieuwe Amstelstraat **121/D5**
Nieuwe Batavierstraat **121/E4**
Nieuwe Doelenstraat **120/B5-C5**
Nieuwe Foliestraat **121/F4**
Nieuwe Grachtje **121/E4-F4**
Nieuwe Herengracht **121/D6-F5**
Nieuwe Hoogstraat **120/C4-121/D4**
Nieuwe Jonkerstraat **121/D3**
Nieuwe Keizersgracht **121/D6-E6**
Nieuwe Kerkstraat **128/C1-129/D1**
Nieuwe Nieuwstraat **120/B2**
Nieuwe Prinsengracht **128/C1-129/D1**
Nieuwe Ridderstraat **121/D3**
Nieuwe Spaarpotsteeg **120/A2-B2**
Nieuwe Uilenburgerstraat **121/D4-E4**
Nieuwebrugsteeg **120/C2-121/D2**

Nieuwendammerdijk **124/C1-125/F2**
Nieuwendijk **120/B2-C1**
Nieuwezijds Armsteeg **120/C1-C2**
Nieuwezijds Kolk **120/B2**
Nieuwezijds Voorburgwal **120/A5-B2**
Nieuwpoortstraat **122/A2-B2**
Nobelweg **129/E3-F4**
Noorderkerkstraat **120/A1-YY/A3**
Nova Zemblastraat **123/D1**

O

Obrechtsplein **127/E3**
Okeghemstraat **126/C3-C4**
Oldenbarneveldtstraat, van **122/C4**
Olieslagerssteeg **120/B5**
Olofspoort, Sint **121/D2**
Olympiakade **126/C4**
Olympiaplein **127/D4**
Olympiaweg **126/C5-127/D4**
Omval **120/D5-E5**
Onkelboerensteeg **120/C4**
Onze Lieve Vrouwesteeg **120/B2-C2**
Oosteinde **128/C2**
Oostenburgergracht **124/C5-C6**
Oosterdokskade **121/E2-F2**
Oosterpark **129/E2**
Oosterparkstraat, 1e **128/C3-129/D2**
Oosterparkstraat, 2e **129/D3-E2**
Oosterparkstraat, 3e **129/D3-E2**
Oostersekade **121/E4**
Oostzaanstraat **122/C1**
Openhartsteeg **120/B6**
Oranje Nassaulaan **126/C3**
Oranje Vrijstraatkade **129/F3**
Ostadestraat, van **128/C3**
Oude Doelenstraat **120/C4**
Oude Hoogstraat **120/C4**
Oude Leliegracht **120/A2**
Oude Nieuwstraat **120/B2**
Oude Spiegelstraat **120/A4**
Oude Turfmarkt **120/B5**
Oude Waal **121/D3-E3**
Oudebrugsteeg **120/C2**
Oudekennissteeg **120/C3**
Oudekerksplein **120/C3**
Oudemanhuispoort **120/C4-C5**
Oudeschans **121/D4-E4**
Oudezijds Achterburgwal **120/C4-121/D3**
Oudezijds Armsteeg **120/C2-121/D2**
Oudezijds Kolk **121/D2**
Oudezijds Voorburgwal **120/B4-C3**
Overschiestraat **126/A4-A5**
Overtoom **126/C2-127/E1**

P

Paardenstraat **120/C5-C6**
Paleisstraat **120/A3-B3**
Palmgracht **123/D3**
Panaalsteeg **120/C1**
Panama lan **125/D5-D6**
Panamakade **125/E5-F4**
Papenbroekssteeg **120/B3**
Papenbrugsteeg **120/C3**
Paramaribostraat **126/B1-B2**
Parnassusweg **127/D5-D6**
Pastelstraat **128/B4**
Paternostersteeg **120/C2**
Patroclosstraat **127/D5**

Paulus Potterstraat **127/E2-F2**
Pekstraat, van der **124/A2-B1**
Pentagon **121/D4**
Peperstraat **121/E4-F3**
Piet Heinkade **124/B4-125/D5**
Pieter Cornelisz. Hoofstraat **127/E2-F2**
Pieter Jacobsdwarsstraat **120/B3-B4**
Pieter Jacobszstraat **120/B4**
Pieter Lastmankade **126/C4-127/D3**
Pieter Lodewijk Takstraat **128/B4**
Pieter van der Doesstraat **122/A4-A5**
Pietershalsteeg, Sint **120/B6**
Pieterspoortsteeg, Sint **120/B4**
Piet-Hein-Tunnel **125/D5-F4**
Pijlsteeg **120/B3-C3**
Pilotenstraat **126/A5-A6**
Plantage Badlaan **129/D1**
Plantage Doklaan **121/F5-129/E1**
Plantage Kerklaan **121/F5-F6**
Plantage Lepellaan **129/D1**
Plantage Middenlaan **121/F5-129/E1**
Plantage Muidergracht **121/F6-129/E1**
Plantage Parklaan **121/E6-F5**
Plantage Westermanlaan **129/D1**
Plantagekade **121/F5**
Poeldijkstraat **126/A4**
Poggenbeekstraat **128/B4**
Polanenstraat **123/D1**
Polderweg **129/F2**
Pontanusstraat **129/F1-F2**
Populierenweg **129/D3-E2**
Postjeskade **126/B1-B2**
Postjesweg **126/A1-C1**
Pr. Marijkestraat **127/D5**
President Kennedylaan **128/B6-129/D5**
Pretoriusplein **129/E3**
Pretoriusstraat **129/E3-F3**
Prins Bernhardplein **129/E4**
Prins Hendrikkade **120/C1-ZZ/D5**
Prins Hendriklaan **126/C3-127/D3**
Prinseneiland **123/E2**
Prinsengracht **123/E3-128/C1**
Prinsengracht **123/E3**
Prinsenhofssteeg **120/C4**
Prinsenstraat **120/A1**
Prinses Irenestraat **127/D5-E6**
Prinses Margrietstraat **127/E5**
Purmerhof **125/F1**
Purmerweg **125/E1-F1**

Q

Quelijnstraat **128/A2-B3**

R

Raadhuisstraat **120/A3**
Raamgracht **120/C4-121/D5**
Ramskooi **120/C1**
Ramsteeg **120/A4**
Ranonkelkade **124/A1-A2**
Rapenburg **121/E4-F4**
Rapenburgerplein **121/F4**
Rapenburgerstraat **121/E5**
Raphaelplein **127/D4**
Raphaelstraat **127/D4**
Recht Boomssloot **121/D3**
Reestraat **123/D5**
Reggestraat **128/C4**
Reguliersbreestraat **120/B5-C6**

Reguliersdwarsstraat **120/A5-C6**
Reguliersgracht **128/B1-B2**
Regulierssteeg **120/B5-B6**
Reigersbergenstraat, van **122/C4-C5**
Reijnier Vinkeleskade **127/E3-F4**
Reinaert de Vosstraat **122/A3**
Rembrandtplein **120/C6**
Retiefstraat **129/E3**
Rietwijkerstraat **126/A4-B4**
Rijnsburgstraat **126/B4**
Rijnstraat **128/C4-C6**
Rijpgracht, de **122/B4**
Ringdijk **129/D4-F3**
Ringweg Zuid **126/A6-127/F6**
Roelensteeg Jonge **120/B3**
Roelof Hartplein **127/F3**
Roelof Hartstraat **127/F3**
Roerstraat **128/B5**
Roetersstraat **129/D1**
Rokin **120/B3-B5**
Romeinsarmsteeg **120/A4**
Roomolenstraat **120/B1**
Rooseveltlaan **128/B5-C5**
Rosendaalstraat **129/E5**
Roskamsteeg **120/A4**
Rosmarijnsteeg **120/A4**
Rozengracht **123/D4-D5**
Rubensstraat **127/E4-E5**
Ruijterkade, de **123/F3-124/B4**
Runstraat **123/D5**
Rusland **120/B1**
Rustenburgerstraat **128/A4-C3**
Rusthofstraat **129/D1**
Ruyschstraat **128/C3-129/D2**
Ruysdaelstraat **127/E3-F3**

S
Safflerstraat **128/C4**
Sarphatipark **128/B3**
Sassenheimstraat **126/A4-B4**
Schaafstraat **124/C2**
Schagerlaan **129/E4-E5**
Scheldeplein **128/A5**
Scheldestraat **128/B4-B5**
Schimmelstraat **122/B5**
Schinkelkade **126/B3-B4**
Schippersgracht **121/F4**
Schornsteenvegerssteeg **120/A4**
Schoutensteeg **120/C3**
Schubertstraat **127/E4-E5**
Servetsteeg **120/C3**
Siebbeleshof, J. B. **121/D4**
Singel **120/B1-B5**
Slijkstraat **120/C4**
Slingelandtstraat, van **122/B2-B3**
Sloterdijkerweg **122/A1**
Sloterkade **126/B2-B4**
Smaksteeg **120/B1-C1**
Smaragdplein **128/C4**
Smidsteeg **121/D2**
Snoekjesgracht **121/D4**
Solebaystraat **122/A2-A3**
Spaarndammerdijk **122/C1-123/D1**
Spaarndammerstraat **123/D1-D2**
Spaarpotsteeg **120/B3-B4**
Spaklerweg **129/E6**
Speijkstraat, van **122/B5-B6**
Sperwerlaan **124/B2**
Spilbergenstraat, van **122/A5-A6**
Spinhuissteeg **120/C4**
Spui **120/A5-B5**
Spuistraat **120/A5-B1**
Staalstraat **120/C5**
Stadhouderskade **127/E1-128/C2**
Stadionkade **126/C5-127/E5**
Stadionplein **126/C5**

Staringstraat **126/C1-C2**
Stationsplein **120/C1-121/D1**
Steenhouwerssteeg **120/B3-B4**
Stokerkade **125/F5**
Stoofsteeg **120/C3**
Stormsteeg **121/D3**
Strawinskylaan **127/D6-E6**
Stromarkt **120/B1**
Stuurmankade **125/E5-F5**
Stuyvesantstraat **126/C1**
Suikerbakkerssteeg **120/B2**
Sumatrakade **124/C3-125/E4**
Surinameplein **126/B2**
Surinamestraat **126/B2**
Sweelinckstraat, 1e **128/B3**
Swindenstraat, 2e, van **129/E2-F1**

T
Taksteeg **120/B5**
Talmastraat **128/C4**
Tasmanstraat **123/D1**
Teerketelstraat **120/B1-B2**
Terheideweg **126/A3**
Theophile de Bockstraat **126/A3-B3**
Thorbeckeplein **120/C6**
Thorn Prikkerstraat **126/A1**
Tichelstraat **123/D3-D4**
Tilanusstraat **129/D2**
Titiaanstraat **127/D4**
Tolstraat **128/C3**
Torensteeg **120/A2**
Transformatorweg **122/A1-B1**
Transvaalkade **129/D4-F3**
Transvaalstraat **129/E3-F3**
Treeftsteeg **120/B4**
Trompenburgstraat **128/C5-D5**
Tugelaweg **129/D3-F2**
Turbinestraat **122/A1**
Turfdraagsterpad **120/B5**
Turfsteeg **121/D5**
Tuyll van Serooskerkenplein **127/D5**
Tuyll van Serooskerkenweg **126/C5**

U
Uilenburgersteeg **121/D4-D5**
Uiterwaardenstraat **128/B6-129/D5**
Uithoornstraat **128/C4-129/D4**
Utrechtsestraat **128/B1**

V
Vaartstraat **126/B4-C4**
Valckenierstraat **129/D1**
Valeriusplein **126/C3-127/D3**
Valeriusstraat **126/C4-127/D3**
Valkenburgerstraat **121/D5-F4**
Valkensteeg **120/B3**
Valschermkade **126/A5-A6**
Vechtstraat **128/C4-C6**
Veerstraat **126/C3-C4**
Veluwelaan **128/B6**
Vendelstraat **120/B5-C5**
Verbindingsdam **125/E4**
Verversstraat **120/C5**
Vespuccistraat **122/A4-A5**
Victorieplein **128/C5**
Vierwindenstr. **123/E2**
Vijzelgracht **128/A2-B1**
Vijzelstraat **120/B6-128/B1**
Visseringstraat **122/C3-C4**
Vliegendesteeg **120/A4**
Vliegtuigstraat **126/A6**
Voetboogstraat **120/A5-B5**
Vogelkade **124/C2-125/D2**
Vogelstraat **124/C2-125/D2**

Vondelstraat **127/D2-F1**
Voorburgstraat **126/A4**
Vredenburgersteeg **121/D2**
Vrijheidslaan **128/C5-129/D4**
Vrolikstraat **129/D3-E2**

W
W. Passtorsstraat **128/B4**
Waalstraat **128/B4-C6**
Waddenweg **122/C1-123/D1**
Wagenaarstraat **129/E1-F1**
Wagenstraat **120/C6**
Walbeeckstraat, van **126/B1-B2**
Walenplein **120/C4**
Warmoesstraat **120/B3-C2**
Warmondstraat **126/B2-B3**
Watergangsweg **125/E1-F1**
Waterlooplein **121/D5-D6**
Watersteeg **120/B4**
Waverstraat **128/C5-129/D5**
Weesperstraat **121/E5-128/C2**
Weesperzijde **128/C2-129/D5**
Wenslauerstraat **122/B6**
Westerdoksdijk **123/E1-E2**
Willem de Zwijgerlaan **122/A3-B5**
Windrooskade **124/C5**

Z
Zaandammerplein **123/D1-D2**
Zaanhof **122/C1**
Zaanstraat **122/C1-123/D2**
Zamenhofstr. **125/D2**
Zanddwarsstraat **120/C4-121/D4**
Zandhoek **123/E1-E2**
Zandpad **127/E1-2**
Zandstraat **120/C4-121/D4**
Zeeburgerdijk **125/D6-F6**
Zeeburgerkade **125/E5-F5**
Zeeburgerpad **125/D6-F6**
Zeeburgerstraat **124/C6**
Zeedijk **121/D2-D3**
Zeilstraat **126/B4-C4**
Zesenstraat, Von **129/E1-F1**
Zoutsteeg **120/B3**
Zuidelijke Wandelweg **128/B6-C6**
Zuiderkerkhof **121/D4**
Zuiderzee **125/F6**
Zwanenburgwal **120/C5-129/D5**
Zwarte Handsteeg **120/B2**

KEY TO STREET ATLAS

Autosnelweg / Autobahn		Motorway / Autoroute
Weg met vier rijstroken / Vierspurige Straße		Road with four lanes / Route à quatre voies
Weg voor dorgaand verkeer / Durchgangsverkehr		Thoroughfare / Route de transit
Hoofdweg / Hauptstraße		Main road / Route principale
Overige wegen / Sonstige Straßen		Other roads / Autres routes
Parkeerplaats - Informatie / Parkplatzrk - Information	P i	Parking place - Information / Parking - Information
Straat met eenrichtingverkeer / Einbahnstraße		One way road / Rue à sens unique
Voetgangerszone / Fußgängerzone		Pedestrian zone / Zone piétonne
Belangrijke spoorweg met station / Hauptbahn mit Bahnhof		Main railway with station / Chemin de fer principal avec gare
Overige spoorweg / Sonstige Bahn		Other railway / Autres ligne
Ondergrondse spoorweg / U-Bahn	M	Subway / Métro
Ondergrondse spoorweg in aanleg / U-Bahn in Bau	M	Subway under construction / Métro en construction
Tram - Buslijn / Straßenbahn - Buslinie		Tramway - Bus-route / Tramway - Ligne d'autobus
Autoveer - Veerpont / Autofähre - Personenfähre		Car ferry - Passenger ferry / Bac pour automobiles - Bac pour piétonnes
Aanlegplaats - Sluis / Anlegestelle - Schleuse	⊕ ⊏⊏	Landing stage - Lock / Embarcadère - Écluse
Bezienswaardige kerk - Kerk / Sehenswerte Kirche - Kirche	⊞ ⊞	Church of interest - Church / Église remarquable - Église
Synagoge - Moskee / Synagoge - Moschee	✡ ☾	Synagogue - Mosque / Synagogue - Mosquée
Monument - Politiebureau / Denkmal - Polizeistation	⚑ ●	Monument - Police station / Monument - Poste de police
Postkantoor / Postamt	✍	Post office / Bureau de poste
Ziekenhuis - Jeugdherberg / Krankenhaus - Jugendherberge	✛ ▲	Hospital - Youth hostel / Hôpital - Auberge de jeunesse
Vliegveldbus - Kampeerterrein / Flughafenbus - Campingplatz	B ⛺	Airport bus - Camping site / Bus d'aéroport - Terrain de camping
Windmolen / Windmühle	✶	Windmill / Moulin à vent
Bebouwing - Openbaar gebouw / Bebaute Fläche - Öffentliches Gebäude		Built-up area - Public building / Zone bâtie - Bâtiment public
Industrieterrein - Park, bos / Industriegelände - Park, Wald		Industrial area - Park, forest / Zone industrielle - Parc, bois
Wandelingen door de stad / Stadtspaziergänge		Walking tours / Promenades en ville
MARCO POLO Highlight	★	MARCO POLO Highlight

INDEX

This index lists all sights and excursion destinations featured in this guide, plus the names of some important terms and people, streets and squares. Numbers in bold indicate a main entry.

9 straatjes 68
Ajax Amsterdam **40**
Albert Cuypmarkt 7, 24, 66, 69, **72**
Amstel 11, 13
Amstelkerk **40**
Amsterdam Dungeon **29**
Amsterdam Museum **29**
Amsterdam School 36
Amsterdam (East India ship) **48**
Amsterdamse Bos (woods) 9, 90
Anatomical Theatre 37
Anne Frank Huis **40**, 100
Artis (Zoo) 8, **100**
Begijnhof 29, **30**, 31, **32**, 94
Beurs van Berlage **30**, 82
Blauwbrug **45**
Blijburg aan Zee 9, 54
Botanical garden (Hortus Botanicus) **46**, 47
Canals **18**, 28, 38, 80, 100, 102, 103
Canal gardens 102
Canal Ring 10, 12, 24, 26, **38**, 41, 45, 107, 140
Canal trips **80, 107**
Centraal Station (main station) **32**, 106
Chinatown 6, 13, 25, 28, **32**, 56, 57, 63
Coffee shops 14, **19**, 140
Concertgebouw 5, 6, 49, 77, **82**
Dam 14, 26, 29, 33, 34, 35, 68, 74, 103
De Pijp 4, 24, **49**, 76
Drieharingenbrug 97
Dutch Design 8, **19**, 102
Eye Film Institute 15, **53**
Fiets (bicycle) 7, 15, **18**, 90, 106, 109, 140
Flowers **20**
FOAM **41**
Fo Guang Shan He Hua Temple 6, 32
Gassan Diamonds **45**
Golden Age 6, 13, 14, 24, 26, 30, 38, 47, 48, 50
Gouden Bocht (Golden Arc) 7, **41**, 107
Gouden Reael 97

Haarlemmerdijk 8, 68, 97, 98
Heineken Experience **49**
Hermitage Amsterdam **46**
Hofje (courtyards) 12, **94**, 95, 96, 109
Home cooking 16
Homomonument **42**
Hortus Botanicus (botanical garden) **46**, 47
Houseboats 5, **21**, 85, 97
IJburg 9, **54**
IJ, het 14, **20**, 53, 107
IJsselmeer 13, 18, 20, 54, 109
Java Eiland 98, 99
Jewish quarter 44, **45**, 47
Joods Historisch Museum **47**
Jordaan 6, 12, 24, **38**, 90, 94, 103, 107, 109
Karthuizerhof 96
King Willem Alexander 7, 8, 22, 33, 35, 102
KNSM Eiland 98
Koninklijk Paleis 8, **32**
Leidseplein 11, 12, 25, **42**, 61, 68, 76, 100, 102, 113
Lloyd Hotel 5, **89**, 98
Madame Tussaud's **33**, 49
Magere Brug 7, **42**, 62
Main station **32**, 106
Marken **54**
Martin Luther King Park 103
Monarchy 7, 8, **21**, 33, 35
Montelbaanstoren **33**
Muntplein 68
Munttoren **34**
Museumplein 27, 48, 50, 51, 68, 102
Museum Van Loon **42**, 43
Muziektheater, het **83**
Nationaal Monument **34**
Nemo Science Center 9, 49, **100**
Nieuwe Kerk **34**
Nieuwendam 4, 9, **54**
Nieuwe Suykerhofje 95
Nieuwmarkt 25, 29, 32, **35**, 76
Noorderkerk **42**, 96
Noordermarkt 42, **73**
Oostelijke Haveneilanden (eastern harbour islands) 5, 89, 99

Oosterpark 102
Openbare Bibliotheek (municipal library) 8, **35**, 36
Oude Kerk 34, **36**, 37
Oudezijds Achterburgwal 13, 16
Oud Zuid **49**
Pijp de 4, 24, **49**, 76 Pinto-huis **47**
Piraeus Building 99
Plantage, de **44**
Prinseneiland 97
Queen Beatrix 7, 22, 81
Race Planet For Kids **101**
Raepenhofje 96
Realeneiland 97
Rembrandthuis **47**
Rembrandtplein 12, 29, **43**, 76
Rijksmuseum 13, 14, 24, 26, 27, 43, **50**, 82, 91, 100
Red-light district 16, 29
Scheepstimmermanstraat 98
Scheepvaartgebouw 86
Scheepvaarthuis **36**
Scheepvaartmuseum **48**
Schip, het **54**
Schreierstoren **36**
Schuttersgalerij 6, 29
Secret Church 12, **30**, 35
Sint Andrieshofje 96
Sporenburg peninsula 98
Spui 29, **37**, 76
Stadsschouwburg 59, 76, 77, **83**, 102, 108
Stedelijk Museum 13, 16, 26, 27, **51**
Steigereiland 54
Stopera (Muziektheater and Stadhuis) 45, 83
Tassenmuseum Hendrikje (handbag museum) **43**
Tropenmuseum 8, **49**
Tunfun **101**
Tuschinski **81**, 83
Utrechtsestraat 17, 25, 68
Van Brienenhofje 96
Van Gogh Museum 13, 26, **52**
Venetiaehofje 94

Verenigde Oostindische Compagnie (VOC) 13
Vondelpark 5, 6, 14, 49, **52**, 53, 59, 80, 82, 88, 91, 93, 102
Waag de **37**
Wallen, de 26, **28**

Waterlooplein **44**, 73, 83
Westergasfabriek 58, 64
Westerkerk 15, 24, 26, 42, **44**
Western harbour islands **96**
Westertoren 23, 26, **44**
Westindische Compagnie 13

Whale Building, The 98
Willet Holthuysen Museum **44**
Winkels 13, 68
Zandvoort aan Zee **55**
Zoo (Artis) 8, **100**
Zuiderbad 43

WRITE TO US

e-mail: info@marcopologuides.co.uk

Did you have a great holiday? Is there something on your mind? Whatever it is, let us know! Whether you want to praise, alert us to errors or give us a personal tip – MARCO POLO would be pleased to hear from you. We do everything we can to provide the very latest information for your trip.

Nevertheless, despite all of our authors' thorough research, errors can creep in. MARCO POLO does not accept any liability for this. Please contact us by e-mail or post.

MARCO POLO Travel Publishing Ltd
Pinewood, Chineham Business Park
Crockford Lane, Chineham
Basingstoke, Hampshire RG24 8AL
United Kingdom

PICTURE CREDITS

Cover Photograph: Look: Pompe (Keizersgracht, Leasure Boot)
Photos: M. Beemster (16 top); A. Bokern (1 bottom); DuMont Bildarchiv: Kiedrowski (2 centre top, 6, 9, 30, 38, 43, 52/53, 97, 102, 103); R. Freyer (cover left, 2 centre bottom, 2 bottom, 3 centre, 3 bottom, 12, 14/15, 26/27, 34/35, 37, 47, 56/57, 58, 72, 76/77, 84/85, 94/95, 98/99); Huber: Gräfenhain (54/55); L. Kornblum (60 left, 106 top, 118/119); C. Lachenmaier (7, 61, 70, 91); Laif: Gonzalez (3 top, 24 bottom, 68/69, 78, 81, 89), Modrow (cover right, 106 bottom); Laif/Aurora: Azel (101); Laif/hemis.fr: Maisant (66); Laif/Hollandse Hoogte: Miller (102/103), Schlijper (25); Laif/Hoogte: Holland (93); Laif/RAPHO: Luider (44); Look: Pompe (1 top), Look/SagaPhoto: Forget (75, 83), Gautier (2 top, 4); mauritius images: AGE (100/101), Alamy (8, 16 bottom, 21, 22, 36, 51, 60 right, 63, 65); mauritius images/imagebroker: Gabriel (48), Mateo (18/19), Moxter (5), Zaglitsch (33); Leonard van Munster: René Gerritsen (16 centre); RAWIMG31.COM (17 bottom); Rederij Lovers (17 top); vario images: imagebroker (10/11), Johner Bildbyra (100), RHPL (41, 107); Visum: Zaglisch (24 top); M. Zegers (42, 86)

2nd Edition – revised and updated 2014

Worldwide Distribution: Marco Polo Travel Publishing Ltd, Pinewood, Chineham Business Park, Crockford Lane, Basingstoke, Hampshire RG24 8AL, United Kingdom. Email: sales@marcopolouk.com
© MAIRDUMONT GmbH & Co. KG, Ostfildern
Chief editor: Marion Zorn
Author: Anneke Bokern; Editor: Christina Sothmann
Programme supervision: Ann-Katrin Kutzner, Nikolai Michaelis, Silwen Randebrock
Picture editor: Stefan Scholtz, Gabriele Forst
What's hot: wunder media, Munich
Cartography road atlas: © MAIRDUMONT, Ostfildern
Cartography pull-out map: © MAIRDUMONT, Ostfildern
Design: milchhof: atelier, Berlin; Front cover, pull-out map cover, page 1: factor product munich
Translated from German by John Sykes, Cologne; editor of the English edition: Kathleen Becker, Lisbon
Phrase book in cooperation with Ernst Klett Sprachen GmbH, Stuttgart, Editorial by Pons Wörterbücher

DOS & DON'TS!

Some things are best avoided in Amsterdam

ASSUMING EVERYONE SPEAKS ENGLISH

The Dutch are fantastically good linguists. Most people you meet in tourist places will readily communicate in English, many of them fluently, and they don't expect foreigners to master their own language. Nevertheless, it often pays dividends to show willing by at least learning a few basics like 'thank you', 'good morning' and 'please'.

WALKING ROUND OBLIVIOUS TO TRAFFIC

A lot of visitors seem to think Amsterdam is some kind of huge open-air museum, and wander around the Canal Ring in the middle of the road. This infuriates Dutch drivers and cyclists, who can suddenly turn out to have an almost Mediterranean temperament. If you don't mind where you step, at best you'll be the target of a lot of horn-hooting and bell-ringing, and at worst you'll be knocked over. When you go for a stroll, watch out for cyclists, who often shoot round corners at incredible speed. The rules for bikes are liberal. They can go the wrong way down one-way streets and ride side by side. Official bike paths are marked by red asphalt.

DRIVING INTO THE CITY CENTRE

Amsterdam's city centre is overcrowded, full of roadworks and other construction sites, and the roads are jammed. Along the canals traffic is often blocked by stationary delivery vans. Careless cyclists throng the main roads. Parking spaces are scarce and expensive. As the city centre is compact and can easily be explored on foot, by bike or by tram, there is no good reason to drive in. Save yourself the stress and the parking charges.

LEAVING YOUR BIKE UNLOCKED

If you should be brave enough to take your bicycle to Amsterdam or hire a bike while you are there, bear in mind that the city has a breathtakingly high level of cycle theft. Even a really good lock is not always enough to deter an expert thief, and if the bike is not attached securely to something immovable like a lamppost, you might not see it again.

FALLING FOR OFFERS OF DRUGS

Amsterdam is permissive, but it's by no means true that anything goes. Only so-called 'soft drugs' such as hashish and marihuana are tolerated, and they may only be sold in 'coffee shops' with an official licence. Buying and selling them on the street is prohibited. If you do buy on the street, you risk not only a fine but also being robbed in the nearest dark alley. Import and export of opiates is punishable in the Netherlands by a jail sentence of up to twelve years, and possession or sale of less than 30 g of soft drugs can get you a month in prison.